Going Pro with Logic® Pro 9

Jay Asher

Course Technology PTR
A part of Cengage Learning

COURSE TECHNOLOGY
CENGAGE Learning·

Australia • Brazil • Japan • Korea • Mexico • Singapore • Spain • United Kingdom • United States

COURSE TECHNOLOGY
CENGAGE Learning™

Going Pro with Logic® Pro 9

Jay Asher

Publisher and General Manager,
Course Technology PTR:
Stacy L. Hiquet

Associate Director of Marketing:
Sarah Panella

Manager of Editorial Services:
Heather Talbot

Marketing Manager: Mark Hughes

Acquisitions Editor: Orren Merton

Project Editor/Copy Editor:
Cathleen D. Small

Technical Reviewers: Joey Mosk
and Nick Batzdorf

Interior Layout Tech: MPS Limited,
A Macmillan Company

Cover Designer: Mike Tanamachi

Indexer: Sharon Shock

Proofreader: Sandi Wilson

For product information and technology assistance, contact us at
Cengage Learning Customer & Sales Support, 1-800-354-9706

For permission to use material from this text or product, submit all requests
online at **cengage.com/permissions**

Further permissions questions can be emailed to
permissionrequest@cengage.com

Logic is a registered trademark of Apple Inc., registered in the U.S. and
other countries. All other trademarks are the property of their respective
owners.

All images © Cengage Learning unless otherwise noted.

Library of Congress Control Number: 2009942399

ISBN-13: 978-1-4354-5563-4
ISBN-10: 1-4354-5563-0

Course Technology, a part of Cengage Learning
20 Channel Center Street
Boston, MA 02210
USA

Cengage Learning is a leading provider of customized learning
solutions with office locations around the globe, including Singapore,
the United Kingdom, Australia, Mexico, Brazil, and Japan. Locate your local
office at: **international.cengage.com/region**

Cengage Learning products are represented in
Canada by Nelson Education, Ltd.

For your lifelong learning solutions, visit **courseptr.com**

Visit our corporate website at **cengage.com**

Printed in the United States of America
1 2 3 4 5 6 7 12 11 10

This book is dedicated to my family and friends who have supported and encouraged me throughout my life and career: my lovely, smart, and talented daughter, Emily Marissa; my parents, Sherman and Renee Altshuler; my late grandparents, who I feel are always with me; my aunts and uncles; Jon Feltheimer, who believed in my talent early on and has always been there for me; and my fellow composers and musicians, whose brilliance, creativity, and commitment are a constant inspiration.

Especially, this book is dedicated to my lovely wife, partner, best friend, teacher, soulmate, and self-described computer widow, Rosemary, whose belief in me is my daily sustenance.

Acknowledgments

There are so many people I would like to thank, and I know I am going to miss a few, so please let me apologize in advance if I have omitted mentioning you.

First of all, I would like to thank my friend Orren Merton, who shocked me by offering me the opportunity to write this book, and my terrific and indefatigable editor, Cathleen Small. Thanks are also due to my tech editors, Nick Batzdorf and the brilliant Joey Mosk.

I would also like to thank some folks who gave me technical assistance, constructive criticism, and valuable suggestions: the aforementioned Orren Merton, Christopher Smith, Peter Schwartz, David Nahmani, Steve Horelick, Theo Lovejoy, James Cigler, Ray Colcord, Len Sasso, Ron Aston, Kirk Hunter, David Michael Frank, and Don Gunn.

Thanks is due to several software companies who were very generous in providing me tools for some of the tasks I tackled in this book: Apple Computers, Universal Audio, Native Instruments, East West, and Propellerhead.

Finally, I would like to thank my Emapple friends, some of whom I have known since I first started using C-Lab Notator on the Atari, back when dinosaurs still roamed the earth, and some of whom I have met more recently: Bob Hunt, Dr. Gerhard Lengeling, Chris Adam, Clemens Homburg, Manfred Knauff, Dave Smith, Thorsten Adam, Sascha Kujawa, Panos Kolias, Bill Burgess, and Robert Brock.

About the Author

Jay Asher has had a long and diverse career in the entertainment industry. A Boston native, Jay graduated the Boston Conservatory of Music as a composition major. He moved to Los Angeles in 1972 and studied orchestration with the late Dr. Albert Harris.

Since arriving in Los Angeles, Jay has worked as a composer, songwriter, orchestrator, arranger, conductor, musical director, pianist, and singer for records, TV, film, and live performances. His songs have been recorded by, among others, Mims, Julio Iglesias, Whitney Houston, Donna Summer, Stephanie Mills, and Ahmad Jamal. He has scored TV shows and films, most notably the '90s worldwide hit TV series, *Zorro*.

In recent years, he has added the role of educator to his job description, teaching Logic Pro at UCLA Extension, the Songwriting School of Los Angeles, and as a private consultant to many well-known composers and recording artists. He is a Level 2 Certified Trainer.

Jay is also the author of *Going Pro with Logic Pro 8*.

Contents

Chapter 2
Becoming a Logic Pro 9 Stud: Techniques for Composing
and Editing with Logic Pro 9   49

Chapter 3
Getting in Touch with Your Inner Geek: Techniques for Recording and Mixing with Logic Pro 9   119

Chapter 4
Logic Pro 9 and the Outside World: Techniques for Integrating Third-Party Software and Hardware with Logic Pro 9   157

Introduction

Thank you for your interest in this book. Much to my astonishment, in addition to my career as a composer and musician, I find that I have a career as a Logic Certified Trainer, Level 2, consultant, and now an author. Please believe me when I tell you that I was the *last* guy who was a likely candidate for this. I used to have to call a friend to help me when I wanted to re-patch anything in my studio. But anything is possible with enough desire and some perseverance.

Over the years, I found that there were tasks that I wished to accomplish in Logic that were either not explained or not well explained in the manual, nor were they covered in the two excellent Apple Pro Training books. Also, like most users, there was a wide array of excellent third-party software, plug-ins, and hardware that I wished to make use of to enhance my work, and rarely were there clear step-by-step directions on the best way to do so.

Going Pro with Logic Pro 9 is intended as a small step toward filling that perceived void. It is geared toward Logic Pro users who have a solid grip on the basics of using the application and is not well suited for newbies, as I assume certain basic knowledge. It is a follow-up to my well-received previous book, *Going Pro with Logic Pro 8*. While many of the tutorials are essentially the same as in the previous book but updated for Logic Pro 9, a fair number are entirely new and have replaced other tutorials that enhancements to Logic Pro version 9 rendered unnecessary, in my opinion.

The book consists of 32 tutorials, loosely arranged into four chapters. Chapter 1 deals with topics related to creating customized Logic templates to accomplish specific tasks.

Chapter 2 is centered around techniques for composing and arranging tasks in Logic Pro 9, using its many editing capabilities to tailor the parts to the creator's vision.

Chapter 3 features techniques for recording and mixing these parts. Clearly, there are times when one will be performing these tasks in a different order, depending on the situation and the user's preferred workflow.

Chapter 4 is about efficient methods for using the previously mentioned third-party software and hardware with Logic Pro 9, sometimes within the application and sometimes not. There are thousands of them. My criteria for choosing one was determined by my own use and how often I have been asked by others about the best way to do so. I apologize if I did not get to your favorites.

Logic Pro is an evolving application, and every week there are new products and technological developments by other companies that expand the boundaries of what we can accomplish musically with a computer. It is a constant learning process that I truly enjoy. It is my hope that the readers of this book do as well and that this book is a helpful companion on that journey.

Have fun!

Make It Work: Techniques for Customizing Your Logic Pro 9 Setup for Greater Efficiency

The old saying "an ounce of prevention is worth a pound of cure" certainly applies to Logic Pro 9. The more optimally it is set up for your needs—and it is perhaps the most customizable of all digital audio workstations—the better your experience will be with it. The tutorials in this chapter are designed to help you prepare templates and setups that will help you move down that path.

Tutorial 1: Converting a Logic Pro 7 Template into a Logic Pro 9 (or 8) Template without Headaches

As Logic Pro users well know, we had to wait a long time from Logic Pro 7.2.3 until Logic Pro 8 was finally released, and now, Logic Pro 9. This was not due to laziness on Apple's part. The application, especially the audio engine, has had major changes under the hood.

Many users have one or more templates in Logic Pro 7 that they spent considerable time creating and would like to utilize in Logic Pro 9 or 8. They have tried to do so with varying results.

I have concluded that trying to preserve anything that is related to the audio engine, such as software instruments (formerly audio instruments) and aux/bus schemes, can be problematic. I know; it is a drag. However, preserving MIDI instruments and the Environment layers in which they reside, screensets, text styles, staff styles (formerly score styles), score sets (formerly instrument sets), and so on is not a problem.

Here is an example of the methodology I recommend to safely accomplish this template transition.

Editing and Resaving a Logic Pro Template for Use in Logic Pro 9

Open Logic Pro 7; I am going to assume that you have set it to open an Autoload. This will be the template we will alter, although this will work with any LP7 template, not just the one named Autoload.

1. Logic Pro 9/8 projects cannot be opened in Logic Pro 7, so the first thing you absolutely want to do is save the Autoload under another name. In Logic Pro 8, there is no

Autoload, so you can choose Save As and name it anything you like, perhaps Default Template. Save it to the desktop so you can easily find it.

2. Open the Environment and go to a layer where you keep audio tracks, audio objects, and/ or software instruments, like the one you can see in Figure 1.1.

Figure 1.1   A Logic Pro 7 Environment layer containing audio objects.

3. In the local Options menu, select Layer and then Delete, as you see in Figure 1.2. You will get a warning that there are still objects in the layer and asking whether you want to delete the objects. Sadly, you do. But do not worry—creating audio objects, now channel strips, is *far* easier in LP8/9 than LP7.

4. Now do the same for any other Environment layers that contain audio objects.

5. When you have finished this process, you should have at least two Environment layers left: Clicks & Ports and one or more MIDI Instrument layer(s). If you are like me, the MIDI Instrument layer was the one that took the most time to construct, and the good news is that it is all there.

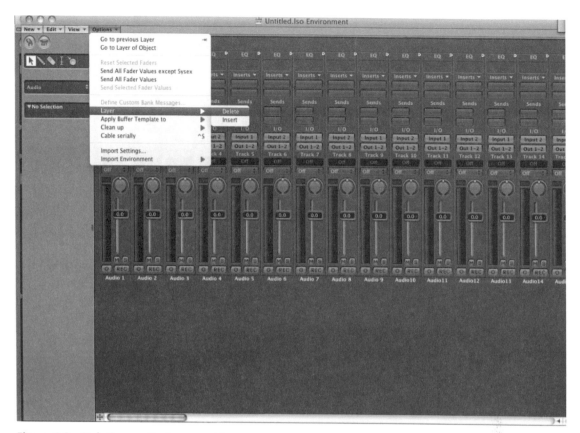

Figure 1.2   Deleting an Environment layer.

6. Return to the Arrange window, and under the local Track menu, choose Delete Unused. If you have MIDI tracks on the Arrange window that you want to preserve, use the Pencil tool to create a blank region on each. See Figure 1.3.

7. Under the Edit menu, scroll down to Delete Undo History. A warning will pop up, asking whether you want to delete all steps and advising you that this cannot be undone. Click Delete. See Figure 1.4.

8. Save again.

The Logic Pro 7 template is now properly prepared to bring into Logic Pro 9. While your audio track, software instrument, aux, and output channel strips will have to be re-created in our new template, everything else has been preserved.

Opening the Template in Logic Pro 9 and Finishing It

Now you will have to repopulate the channel strips you need for audio tracks, software instruments, auxes, and outputs. Hopefully, by now you already know how to do this well in Logic Pro 9, but if not, this should be instructive.

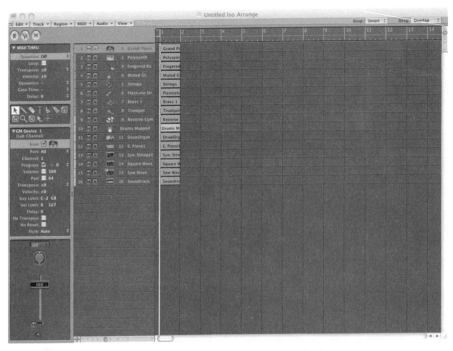

Figure 1.3   Deleting unused tracks from the Arrange window.

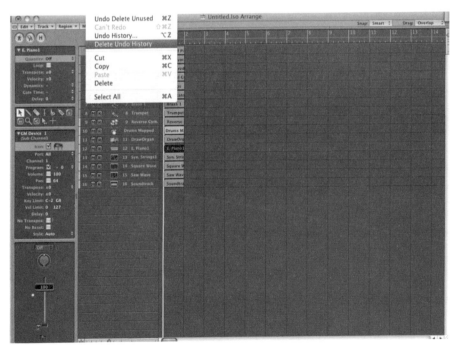

Figure 1.4   Deleting the Undo History.

1. Open Logic Pro 9, and if you have set its preferences to open a project, simply close the project.

2. Open the revised and renamed Logic Pro 7 template.

3. In the Arrange window, above the track list, click the plus sign, and a dialog box for channel strip creation appears. Let's create 16 mono audio tracks. See Figure 1.5.

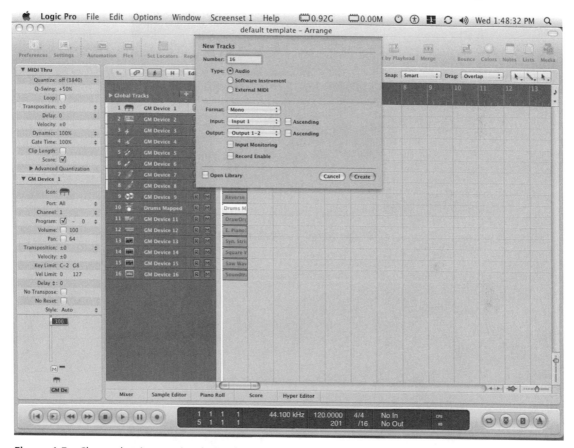

Figure 1.5   Channel strip creation in Logic Pro 9.

4. The tracks are now in the Arrange window, and if you open the Mixer, you will see them there also, as in Figure 1.6.

5. Open the Environment, and you will also find them on an unnamed layer. You could name the layer Mixer as Logic Pro 8 does in its templates, but I would name it Audio, because I like to keep my software instruments on different Environment layers than audio tracks, auxes, outputs, and so on. See Figure 1.7.

6. The same method can now be applied to creating software instruments and their specific auxes, other auxes, outputs, and so on. If you are like me, you will want to keep the

Figure 1.6   The Arrange window with the added audio tracks also reflected in the Mixer.

Figure 1.7   The newly created audio Environment layer.

software instruments and their related auxes on their own layer(s) while auxes and outputs can happily share a layer with the audio tracks. So if you create them with the plus sign, you need to be cognizant of where they end up in the Environment. It is your choice.

7. Follow the same methodology and create the software instruments, auxes, and outputs you would like in your template.

8. Under the File menu, choose Save as Template.

You now have successfully transformed your Logic Pro 7 Autoload template into a working, trouble-free Logic Pro 9 template.

Tutorial 2: Using Software Instruments That Are Both Multi-Timbral and Multi-Output

Multi-timbral software instruments are those that have the ability to direct different sounds/patches to different MIDI channels in the same instance. Multi-output software instruments are those that have the ability to direct sounds/patches to different outputs that are accessed through auxes in Logic Pro 9. While Logic Pro 8's included software instruments are not multi-timbral, with the exception of the EVB3, or multi-output, with the exceptions of the EXS24 and Ultrabeat, many third-party software instruments are, and it may be advantageous to use them as such.

Why multi-timbral? Because today's Macs are such powerhouses that CPU has become less of an issue and RAM access more of an issue, this mostly comes down to workflow choices. If you use Kontakt 4 or 3.5 and are availing yourself of its Memory Server feature, it may make more sense, IMHO, to use separate stereo instances, as in a multi-timbral instance, all the instruments loaded into it are assigned to one core. Indeed, East West goes so far as to recommend using separate stereo instances of its Play-based libraries for this reason. With an instrument such as Spectrasonics' Stylus RMX, which is neither all that CPU intensive nor a big RAM user and has its own mixer and FX built in, I think it clearly makes sense to use it as a multi-timbral software instrument. While it comes down to individual preferences, decisions based on knowing your rig and its plug-ins' RAM demands will yield better performance.

Why multi-output? When you are mixing, particularly with drums and percussion software instruments, it is good to have control of the separate sounds by having them come up on auxes for adding FX and automating. While most of these software instruments do have internal mixing schemes, you are limited to their FX, and automating the software instrument's volume and panning affects all the MIDI channels.

Previous versions of Logic Pro made this task very cumbersome, but Logic Pro 8/9 has made it a lot easier. That said, judging from the many questions I receive about this topic, many users still do not have a grasp on this.

I am going to demonstrate this using Stylus RMX, because it is so popular and, IMHO, it is perhaps the must-have third-party software instrument for anyone working in contemporary music.

Creating a Multi-Timbral, Multi-Output Stylus RMX and Assigning Sounds to MIDI Channels

Creating a multi-timbral software instrument is very easy in LP9.

1.   Open a new Empty Project and when the dialog box appears, choose Software Instrument, check the box for Multi-Timbral, and type 8 for 8 MIDI channels (see Figure 2.1). You will now see eight Inst 1 tracks in your Arrange window, each assigned to a different MIDI channel.

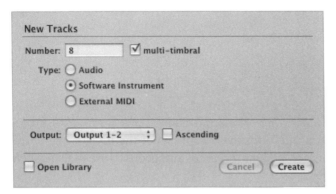

Figure 2.1   The Track Creation dialog box.

2. On any one of these tracks, in the I/O rectangle, hold down the mouse button and guide it to the multi-output version of Stylus RMX. The GUI (*graphical user interface*) will open, since they are all representing the same software instrument.

3. Presumably, those of you who have and use Stylus RMX know how to assign eight loops or sounds to each MIDI channel, so we are going to take the easy way out and load in a prebuilt multi provided by the good folks at Spectrasonics.

4. Click on the Mixer tab, then the floppy disk icon, and navigate to Multi Open > Factory Multis > Cinematic Energy > 090-El Diablo. It loads six loops assigned to MIDI channels 1–6. See Figure 2.2. Play and listen. Cool!

5. (Optional) For those of you who are Stylus RMX savvy, you can drag the loops one at a time from the GUI on the different software instrument tracks in the Arrange window. For those of you who do not own Stylus RMX or have not yet learned this, do not worry about this step.

6. While Stylus RMX is still playing, close the GUI and open the Mixer tab. You will see the signal hitting the channel strip. Now we need to create some auxes on which to bring up Stylus RMX parts. (If listening to it over and over starts to drive you crazy while performing the next steps, simply mute the output.)

Creating Auxes for the Multi-Output Software Instrument and Assigning the Outputs in the Software Instrument

Software instrument aux creation is so easy in Logic Pro 9. All you need to do is click a plus sign (+), but you must click the correct one, and that is where people often go wrong. You want the plus sign that is actually on the Inst 1 channel strip, either in the Inspector or in the Mixer, not the larger one to the left of it. See Figure 2.3.

Figure 2.2   Stylus RMX's Mixer tab with a Factory Multi loaded.

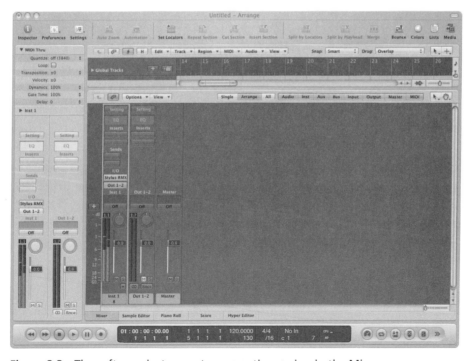

Figure 2.3   The software instrument aux creation + sign in the Mixer.

1. Click the + sign, and an aux will be created with its input assigned to the first available output in the software instrument—in this case, Stylus RMX 3-4, as RMX uses only stereo outputs. (Other software instruments may use only mono or allow you to combine stereo and mono.)

    Repeat this process as many times as possible, depending on how many outputs the software instrument is capable of or you wish to implement. In this case, it is seven. You should now see what is reflected in Figure 2.4.

Figure 2.4   The Mixer with the created auxes for the software instrument.

Fine and dandy, but the sounds are still coming up on the main fader, not the auxes, because we have not assigned the parts to the outputs. The steps we are about to take are similar in every multi-output software instrument, although obviously each GUI will look quite different.

2. Open the Stylus RMX GUI again and go to the Mixer tab. If possible, try to position the GUI on the screen so you can view both it and the Mixer. Notice that directly to the right of each MIDI channel number is an Output assignment rectangle. All six parts are assigned to Output A.

3. Assign the parts for MIDI channels 1–6 to Outputs B–G. (We do not use Output A as it will come up on the main software instrument channel strip instead of an aux, as it is reserved to be a master out.) See Figure 2.5. Close the plug-in.

Figure 2.5   Outputs assigned in the Mixer tab of Stylus RMX.

Now as it is playing back, the sounds are coming up on Inst 1's Auxes 1-5, and we have discrete control for mixing. There are two unused auxes in the Mixer, which you can highlight and simply delete. You can also delete the track for MIDI channel 8 in the Arrange window, because it is not being used.

4.   For automation purposes, you will now want to automate the auxes, because as I wrote earlier in the tutorial, any track-based volume and pan automation you do on the multi-timbral tracks will affect the software instrument as a whole, not discretely. (In all candor, this is an area where, in my humble opinion, Logic could stand some improvement, but Apple's attitude appears to be that with the ever-increasing power of computers, opening multiple instances of software instruments is fine, and multi-timbral use is not that important.) So, in the Mixer, highlight the auxes, and in the local Options menu, choose Create Arrange Tracks for Selected Channel Strips. See Figure 2.6.

We now have created a software instrument that is both multi-timbral and multi-output, and all its parts are being sent to discrete outputs coming up on auxes, which have been added to the Arrange window for mixing and automation! See Figure 2.7.

You may wish to save this project, because I will be using it as the basis for Tutorial 3.

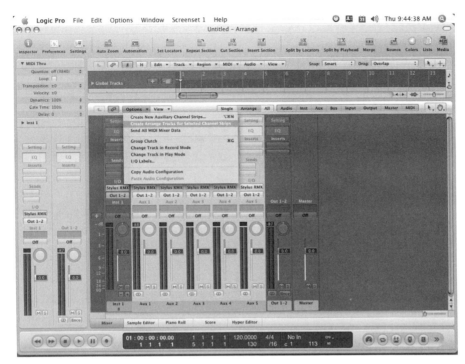

Figure 2.6   In the Mixer, creating Arrange tracks for the software instrument's auxes.

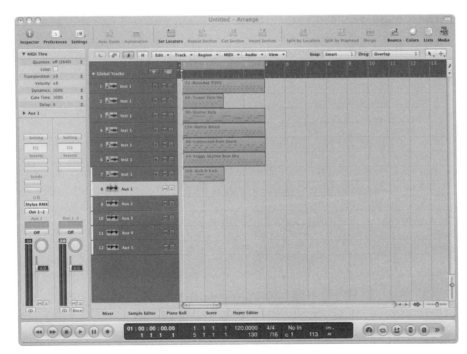

Figure 2.7   The completed Arrange window.

Tutorial 3: Converting Multi-Output Software Instruments to Audio Files

For those of us composing with lots of software instruments, there sometimes is a need to turn the MIDI software instrument tracks into audio files, sometimes called *stems* in the film/TV world. This need may arise when:

- You are going to take the tracks to another studio to be mixed by an engineer, and the studio may not have all the same software instruments or may use a different DAW, such as Pro Tools.

- Your computer is not the latest and greatest, and it is starting to have CPU issues.

- You are like me, and when it comes to mixing audio tracks and software instruments, you prefer to mix Apples with Apples (pun intended), so to speak.

No problem, you say, simply go under the File menu and choose Export > All Tracks as Audio Files. And a fine solution it is, except:

1.   It will not include any volume or panning automation.

2.   If it is a multi-output software instrument and you have assigned different parts to different outputs coming up on auxes, you will not have discrete parts, but a stereo file.

Prior to Logic Pro 7, you had a big problem. If you wanted discrete audio files without the volume and pan automation, you had to de-mix the part by note pitch so that each file was on a different track and then, one at a time, choose Export > Track as Audio File. If you wanted the volume and pan automation included, you had to use Soundflower outputs and inputs as part of an aggregate device, as explained in the "Using Kontakt as a Standalone" tutorial, to route the auxes to audio tracks to record.

Even in LP8, you had to route the output of auxes to the input of audio tracks and record them, as I described in *Going Pro with Logic Pro 8*.

This is now so simple in Logic Pro 9 that this will be quite a short tutorial.

For the purpose of this tutorial, I am using the project with Stylus RMX that I created in Tutorial 2, "Using Software Instruments That Are Both Multi-Timbral and Multi-Output."

1.   Open the project that you saved from following Tutorial 2 or re-create it.

2.   In the Transport bar, set the length of the project to, for example, 33 bars.

3.   Select all the regions (Command+A) and press L to loop them. You should now have a project that looks something like Figure 3.1.

   The other obvious benefit to doing this is that you do not have to have previously automated the auxes. You can do so after the fact with the created audio files.

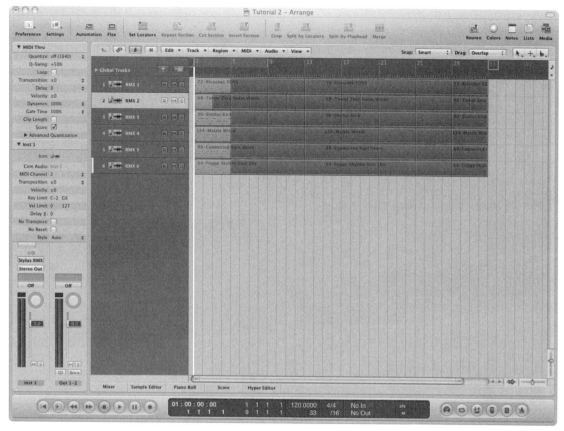

Figure 3.1 A multi-timbral, multi-output RMX with looped MIDI regions in the Arrange area.

4.   Make sure that all the regions are still selected. Under the local Track menu, scroll down to Bounce-Replace All Tracks (see Figure 3.2). You will get an alert suggesting you might wish to save this project first. Not a bad idea.

A dialog box for this task will open, allowing you options to bypass effect plug-ins, include volume and pan automation, and normalize choices. See Figure 3.3.

5.   Click OK, and it does indeed "Bounce-Replace All Tracks." The MIDI tracks and regions in the Arrange area have been replaced by audio tracks with audio files, as is evident in Figure 3.4.

You may now wish to un-instantiate Stylus RMX and/or delete or mute and hide the multi-output software instrument–related tracks for the purpose of mixing the audio files or burn them onto a CD or DVD to bring to another studio.

That's it!

Figure 3.2   Bounce-Replace All Tracks in the Track menu.

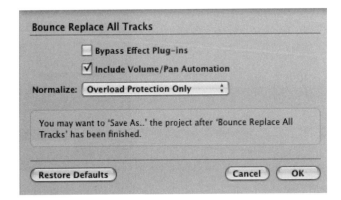

Figure 3.3   The Bounce Replace All Tracks dialog box.

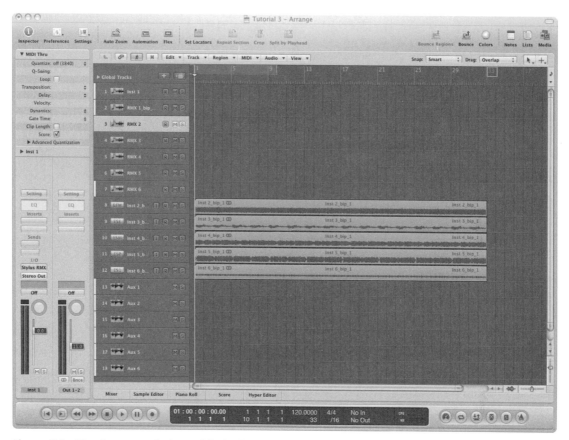

Figure 3.4   The Arrange window with the bounced files added.

Tutorial 4: Customizing an Environment Layer for a "Live" Mixer

With Logic Pro 9, Apple has done a splendid job of both making the Mixer more flexible and making it not as necessary to create channel strips in the Environment.

Many longtime users, however, still prefer to customize Environment layers for specific mixing purposes. In this tutorial, we will create a "live" mixer for bringing seven tracks into LP9 using input channel strips.

Most often, while we may monitor though software FX while recording vocals, guitars, MIDI hardware, and so on, we do not wish to "print" them, which is the old analog console/tape recorder term for marrying the FX to the recording.

But what if we do?

Input Channel Strips

The LP9 manual says, "Additional channel strip types, such as busses and inputs, can also be shown (in the Mixer), but their inclusion is primarily for compatibility with projects created in earlier Logic Pro versions." I say, "Not so fast!"

Let's imagine a scenario in which you are recording simultaneously a singer you want to record with the Logic Delay Designer and Compressor; a guitarist you want to record with Amp Designer and Pedalboard; a bass player using Bass Amp; and a V-Drums player, who is coming out of the V-Drums module, with kit pieces assigned to four outputs, all to be compressed. They are all coming into seven inputs of your audio interface, either directly or through the busses of a console/mixer. You need only add the FX to audio tracks assigned to those inputs to record them while hearing them monitored through the FX, but if you want them to be actually a part of the recording, you still need to create input channel strips in the Environment.

Creating Input Channel Strips

So, let's create the aforementioned input channel strips.

1. Open a new empty project and create seven mono audio tracks assigned to ascending inputs. These are where the recordings will actually be placed. See Figure 4.1.

2. You need to create input channel strips. Look at Figure 4.1 again. Under Type, do you see Input? Sadly, no. You need to create at least one input channel strip in the Environment.

3. To create the input channel strip in the Environment, press Command+8 to open the Environment, and if it does not default to a layer named Mixer, navigate to it by clicking on left pop-up menu. It should appear as it does in Figure 4.2.

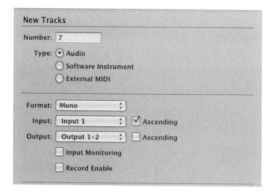

Figure 4.1   The Track Creation dialog box.

Figure 4.2   The Mixer Environment layer with the created audio track channel strips.

4.   Under the Environment's local menu, named New, choose Channel Strip > Input, and an input channel strip will be added to the Mixer Environment layer (see Figure 4.3). Resize the Environment and Arrange windows so that you can drag the Input 1 to the Arrange window's track list under the audio tracks.

Figure 4.3   Creating an input channel strip.

5.   Temporarily, let's close the Environment window.

6.   Either under the Arrange window's local Track menu or by the key command Option+Command+X, you now want to perform Create with Next Channel Strip/Instrument six times.

7.   Open the Environment window. The seven input channel strips are now in the Mixer layer. Let's put them underneath the audio track channel strips in this layer. Rubber-band over the seven input channel strips and double-click on a fader to set them to 0.0 dB.

8. While they are still all selected, drag them down and to the left to position them under the audio track channel strips. Depending on the size of your monitor, you may have to drag down the vertical scroll bar on the right a couple of times to accomplish this. (Alternatively, you could have the input channel strips on their own layer.)

9. Rename the inputs to conform to our scenario using the Text tool. Option-click the faders to set them to a détente value of 0.0 dB. Your Environment layer should now look like Figure 4.4.

Figure 4.4   The Mixer Environment layer with the added input channel strips.

10. All that remains now is to add the desired FX to inserts on the inputs. The end result should look like Figure 4.5.

Now you can arm your audio tracks or, better yet, use LP9's Input Monitoring buttons, represented by the I on the channel strips, play the instruments and adjust the levels being sent to the inputs on your console, mic pres, amps, direct boxes, and so on to get proper levels. See Figure 4.6

You are ready to record using software FX! This method is also a good way to incorporate outboard FX units, simply by patching them into the inputs of your audio interface and inserting I/O plug-ins in inserts on input channel strips.

Figure 4.5   The Mixer Environment layer with the FX in inserts on the input channel strips.

Figure 4.6   The audio tracks with monitoring enabled.

Tutorial 5: Creating an EXS24 Instrument Loader Project

Even with the popularity of libraries for Kontakt, Play, and other competing samplers, for many of us who use large orchestra libraries, the EXS24 is still the first choice.

Why? Kirk Hunter, creator of several excellent orchestral sample libraries for the EXS24, says, "As a sample library developer, I am faced with many options these days where choosing a format is concerned. One of the platforms I have chosen to earnestly support is Apple Logic's EXS24. A big reason I chose EXS24 is simply the way EXS24 sounds. In particular, the default setting of its release envelope is the most natural I've ever heard. And in my opinion, this alone makes for a very natural sound. And when it comes to adding instruments to your arrangement, EXS24 doesn't require any 'multi' setup. You can throw as many EXS instruments at your sequence as your rig will allow...and this can be literally *hundreds* since you're only initiating *one* EXS engine for the whole lot. And while EXS24 might not be as feature-laden as some of the others platforms out there, it most certainly can accomplish what I want a sample playback engine to do for an orchestral library. And mind you, I program very sophisticated instruments! In addition to all of this, it performs everything more efficiently in terms of CPU usage and memory than *anything* I have encountered."

The EXS24 was the first Macintosh-compatible software sampler to use disk streaming to allow it to load large sample sets into RAM quickly when you have the Virtual Memory preference enabled (default) in the EXS24. However, the first time you load up an EXS24 instrument, it takes quite a bit longer than it will subsequently, so after installation, I like to load up all the instruments one time through. It is a big drag, though, to keep having to hit the plus sign in the EXS24's GUI or whatever key command you may assign to it.

The solution is to set up a Logic project that will do it automatically.

Preparing an EXS24 to Change Instruments by Playing a Note

1. Open a Logic Pro 9 Empty Project template with just one software instrument track.

2. Instantiate a mono EXS24 on the newly created channel strip.

3. Under the EXS24's Options menu, choose Preferences, as you see in Figure 5.1.

4. In the Next Instrument pop-up, hold down the mouse and navigate to Note.

5. In the pop-up immediately to the right, choose a note. I recommend either a low note or a high one that you will not accidentally hit on your keyboard, but any note will do. I am choosing C0. See Figure 5.2.

6. Manually load the first EXS24 instrument in the library.

The EXS24 itself is ready to go. Now we will create a MIDI region with the notes to cycle and automatically load each instrument.

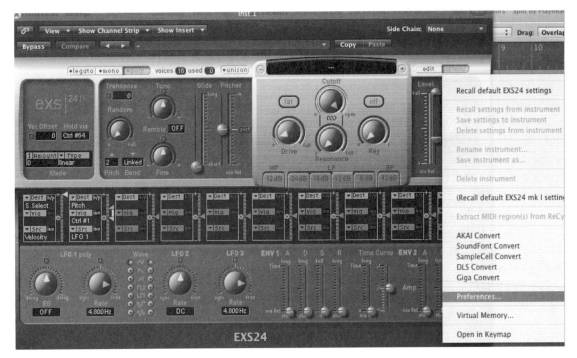

Figure 5.1   Choosing the EXS24's Preferences in its GUI.

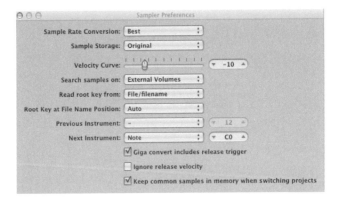

Figure 5.2   An example of Next Instrument in the EXS24's Preferences, assigned to a note.

Creating a MIDI Region for Cycling and Automatically Loading New EXS24 Instruments

Although this region could actually be any length, because we will be cycling it, I chose to create an eight-bar MIDI region.

1.   With the Pencil tool, create a blank region and drag its lower-right corner to resize it eight bars.

2. Open the region in your MIDI editor of choice. Click the MIDI In button so that it turns red, signaling that it is step input ready, as you see in Figure 5.3. You may also want to turn MIDI out off while inputting the notes.

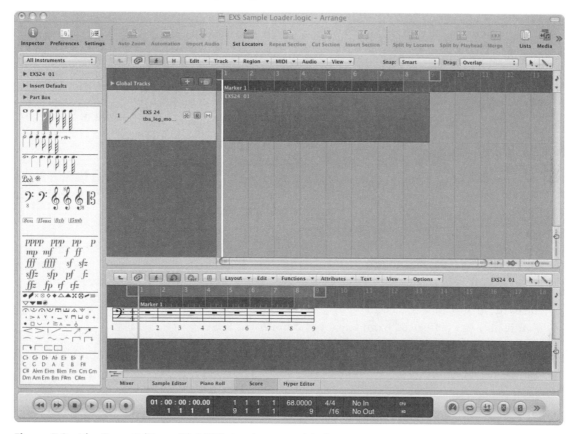

Figure 5.3   The Score Editor with MIDI step input enabled.

The next step can be accomplished by either playing in the notes or step entering. For this tutorial, we will step enter it with the Step Input Keyboard.

3. Under Logic's Options window, choose Step Input Keyboard. Assign its note entry value to a half note, as you see in Figure 5.4.

4. Now you can simply click the mouse button on the C0 key of the Step Input Keyboard 16 times. (Remember, the eight-bar length was an admittedly arbitrary choice.)

5. Turn off the MIDI In button in the MIDI editor you chose. Close the Step Input Keyboard and, if you wish, the MIDI editor also.

Only three easy steps remain to perform.

6. Cycle the project for the length of the region—in this case, eight bars.

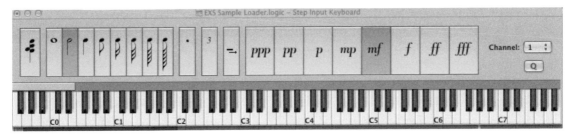

Figure 5.4   The Step Input Keyboard with a step input value of a half note assigned.

7.   In the Transport, double-click the tempo indicator and type in a slow tempo, such as 66.

8.   Hit Play.

Your project will now automatically cycle and continue to load in new instruments. In theory, you can now leave your computer and attend to whatever tasks you would like to attend to. In reality, however, you want to keep an eye on the computer because:

■   Some sample libraries have either duplicate or similarly named samples, and Logic might ask you which one you want to use.

■   Some libraries have hierarchies that require you to manually advance the EXS24 to the first one of the group, or it will go to the wrong one. This is particularly true in my experience with sample libraries converted from GigaStudio libraries.

■   Logic Pro 9 has been known on occasion to unexpectedly quit. You are on a computer; stuff happens. Deal with it.

Tutorial 6: Creating an Orchestral Template in Logic Pro 9 with Third-Party Libraries for the EXS24

Some things have changed since I wrote about this in my Logic Pro 8 book. One is the ascendancy of Native Instruments' Kontakt. Since version 3.5, Kontakt has had the ability to address memory outside its host, advanced scripting capabilities, and of course, it can be run outside of Logic Pro in a supplemental host or as a standalone, both of which topics are covered elsewhere in this book. Finally, many wonderful libraries rely on Kontakt's advanced and recently enhanced scripting capabilities and therefore are only available for Kontakt, such as Audiobro's Los Angeles Scoring Strings.

That said, for running orchestral instruments inside Logic Pro 9, my "go to" is still third-party orchestral libraries for the EXS24. Due to the terrific CPU efficiency of the EXS24, its seamless integration in Logic Pro 9, and its ability to access nearly unlimited available RAM on your computer, it is well suited to the tasks of orchestral mockups, either for sketching and printing out parts for real orchestras or for orchestral simulation.

While one certainly can use orchestral instruments for the EXS24 that are included in the Logic Pro 8 content that are adequate, if you are more serious about this, you are going to want one or more of the excellent orchestral libraries that either are EXS24 or can be converted to it from GigaStudio, and so on. They range from very expensive to quite affordable. For this tutorial, I am using Kirk Hunter's Diamond Orchestra.

There are two ways to approach this task. One is to simply load up a very large number of EXS24s with all the articulations and have them all available in the Arrange window. If you have a great deal of screen real estate, that approach is fine, and I have many friends who choose this. If your libraries of choice have extensive key-switching abilities, as the Diamond Orchestra with its TVEC instruments does, I personally think this makes more sense.

Creating the EXS24 Software Instruments and Optimizing Their Performance

You may well want to have different-size templates for different kinds of projects and different library combinations. Also, depending on the library choices, different users are going to have differing ideas as to just how many EXS24s they will need. One size definitely does not fit all.

A typical template might well include the following: Piccolo; two Flutes; one Oboe; two Clarinets; one Bass Clarinet; one English Horn; one Bassoon; one Contra Bassoon; three Trumpets; three French Horns; three Trombones, including a Bass Trombone; one Tuba; a Harp; a Piano; several percussion instruments, such as Glockenspiel, Piatti, Snare Drums, Timpani, and so on; 1st Violins; 2nd Violins; 1st Violas, 1st Cello; Bass.

So I am going to create 32 software instrument tracks.

1.   Open a Logic Pro 9 Empty Project template with 32 software instrument tracks.

2. In the Mixer on the first software instrument track, load an EXS24 and do not load any EXS24 instrument into it.

3. Open up the GUI and under the Options menu, choose Virtual Memory, as you see in Figure 6.1. There are some choices available here that are new in Logic Pro 9 that we will explore.

Figure 6.1   The Virtual Memory dialog box.

4. Make sure that the Active check box is checked. If you hold down the mouse on the External Memory Area, you will see choices to give memory addressing priority to the EXS24, third-party software instruments that address memory outside the host, or neither. For this template we are creating, we will give precedence to the EXS24. See Figure 6.2.

5. Two things to remember: If you change this setting, you then need to click Apply; this is a preference, so it applies to all projects. If you are working in a project that has fewer EXS24 and more third-party instruments, you will want to change this setting.

6. Now use the Hand tool and hold the Option key down to copy the EXS24 to each of the 33 other software instrument tracks. This may sound like a colossal PITA to do, and, well, it is, but I just did it in one minute and six seconds.

Figure 6.2   The External Memory Area optimized for the EXS24.

Now it is time to load in the patches. This is an area where LP8/9 has made things much easier than in previous versions of Logic Pro.

1.   Select Inst 1 in the Arrange window and click on the Media area and then the Library tab. You will now see all your libraries that are available to load into the EXS24, as you see in Figure 6.3.

2.   In the Mixer, on Audio 1, change its output assignment to Bus 1, and an aux will be created with Bus 1 as its input.

3.   Now you will need to guide with the mouse through the lower hierarchies of the library to get to the patches you desire. With this library, I must navigate to KH Ruby Files Exs > 03 Ruby Woodwinds > Woodwind Solos > Piccolo. Now I see all the EXS24 instruments that come with the Library, as you can see in Figure 6.3.

4.   Since I want keyswitched instruments for their versatility, all I need to do is click on one, and it gets loaded into the EXS24 and renames the track.

5.   Do the same for the remaining 31 instruments.

LP9 has named the tracks in accordance with whatever settings are chosen in the track header configuration, which defaults to Auto Name. So I now have a Track 1 named 00_pc_k_mod Vib,

Figure 6.3   The available libraries displayed in the Library tab of the Media area.

which tells me that it is a piccolo patch that employs key switching and control of the vibrato with the mod wheel. Now, you may be perfectly content with that. I am not.

1.   In the Arrange window's View menu, choose Configure Track Header.

2.   Under Names, switch from Auto Name to Track Name, and it will return to Inst 1, as it was before we loaded in the sampler instrument. That is not what I want, though it may be what you want.

3.   The remaining choices are Channel Strip Setting Name, Software Instrument Setting Name, Channel Strip Name, and Channel Strip Type and Number. Unfortunately, none of them is what I want, although one or the other may be what you want.

Call me crazy, but I want Inst 1 to be named Piccolo, Inst 2 to be named Flute 1, Inst 3 to be named Flute 2, and so on.

1.   Open the Mixer. Double-click on the first channel strip fader and type in Piccolo. Do the same for the remaining channel strips. See Figure 6.4.

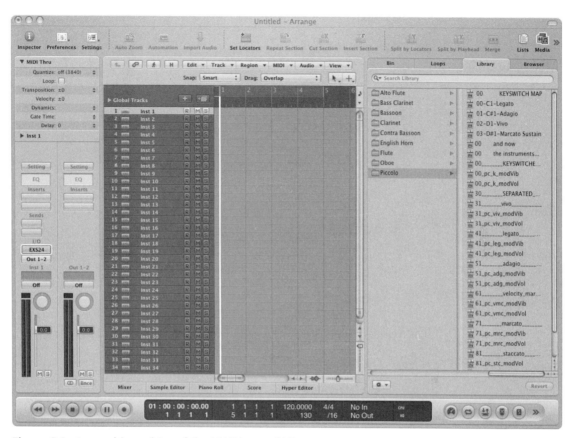

Figure 6.4   Lower hierarchies of the KH Diamond Library.

2.   Close the Mixer and notice that the tracks are named the same way as in the Mixer, as you see in Figure 6.5.

All that remains is to save it as a template, and you are ready to compose. See Figure 6.6.

Some Considerations

There are a lot of things to consider with this kind of template that I am frequently asked.

Q. When do I use a stereo EXS24 and when do I use a mono?

A. There are a lot of different opinions on this, and it depends on a lot of things. Clearly, a flute, for instance, is a mono instrument, so you would probably assume you should choose a mono EXS24. However, most sample libraries have stereo samples, so there really is not a lot of advantage to choosing a mono EXS24, necessarily. That said, I do tend to use them for woodwinds.

Q. Should I pan the instruments according to where they sit on the stage?

A. Some of the libraries are recorded in stereo with the instruments in their standard positions.

Figure 6.5   The Mixer with renamed EXS24 instruments.

Figure 6.6   The Arrange window with renamed EXS24 instruments.

Also, some third-party reverbs, such as Altiverb, have instrument stage positioning available. And of course, orchestras recorded on scoring stages do not necessarily follow the concert paradigms. So, it is strictly a judgment call. If it sounds good, it is good.

Q. Am I better off using just one library at a time or mixing in different instruments from different libraries?

A. Mixing libraries will frequently give you a heightened realism, but not all will blend well together. Once again, if it sounds good, it is good.

Tutorial 7: Customizing Environment Layers for Mixing in Your Orchestral Template in Logic Pro 9

Since Logic Pro 7, Apple has moved us in the direction of using the Mixer for all of our mixing purposes, and this is even more true in Logic Pro 8/9, where we now have more choices as to what we see. However, for customizability, you still cannot top using Environment layers because you can move the channel strips around the page, view only certain ones on certain layers, and so on, and many of us Logic "old-timers" still like this, especially for orchestral simulation work.

I use four layers: Woodwinds, Brass, Strings, and Percussion.

Creating the Environment Layers

I am going to create four Environment layers.

1. If you have not already done so, open your Orchestral template.

2. Hit Command+8 to open your Environment or choose it with the mouse under Logic's large Windows menu. It will probably default to the Mixer layer, showing you any audio-related channel strips, such as software instruments, audio tracks, auxes, and so on that you have already created. See Figure 7.1.

Figure 7.1   A Mixer Environment layer.

3. In the upper left of the layer, where you see the word "Mixer," is a disclosure triangle. If you hold the mouse button down, you will see some choices, including Create Layer, as shown in Figure 7.2.

Figure 7.2   Create Layer in the Environment.

4. Create the layer, and it comes up as (unnamed). Double-click on the word "unnamed" in the rectangle and name it Woodwinds.

5. Repeat the same process for layers for Brass, Strings, and Percussion.

Moving the Software Instrument Channel Strips to the Desired Environment Layers

This is a much easier task than you might expect. We will now move the EXS24 instruments that are playing our woodwind sounds to our newly created Woodwinds Environment layer.

1. Return to the Mixer Environment layer.

2.   Either rubber band or Shift-select the desired instruments. See Figure 7.3.

Figure 7.3   The selected EXS24 instruments in the Mixer layer.

3.   While holding down the Option key, navigate in the disclosure triangle to the Wood-winds layer.

Voila! The EXS24 instruments that are playing the woodwinds sounds are now on a dedicated Woodwinds layer. See Figure 7.4.

If you have a reverb that allows stage placement, as Audio Ease's Altiverb does, or even if you are using Space Designer and want to have more control, you might want to add an aux with the reverb assigned to a bus for mixing purposes in each layer.

1.   On any one of the EXS24 instruments in your Woodwinds layer, choose Sends and, holding down the mouse button, choose Bus 1. This will create an aux with Bus 1 as its input. Done, so why don't I see it? Here in the Woodwinds Environment layer?

Unfortunately, LP9 is going to create it in the Mixer Environment layer, which is not where we want it, so now we have to go through the process of moving it to the proper layer.

Figure 7.4   The Woodwinds layer with the desired EXS24 instruments.

2.   As before, return to the Mixer Environment layer and select Aux 1, as you see in Figure 7.5.

3.   While holding down the Option key, navigate in the disclosure triangle to the Woodwinds layer, and as before, the channel strip will be moved to the desired Environment layer. What? I don't see it!

4.   Use the scroll bar at the bottom of the window to navigate to the right, and there it is. That is not very ergonomically desirable.

5.   Use Command+A to select all the channel strips in the layer.

6.   In the layer's local Options window, navigate to Clean Up > Align Objects (see Figure 7.6). Drag the scroll bar to the left, and you will see the channel strips aligned in a tidy layer for mixing. Add your reverb to the aux, and your Woodwinds layer is complete. See Figure 7.7.

Follow the same process for layers for Brass, Strings, and Percussion. This sounds a lot more complicated and time consuming than it actually is. It can literally be done in a matter of minutes.

Save it as your orchestral template, overwriting the original, and you are good to go!

Figure 7.5   Aux 1 selected in the Mixer Environment layer.

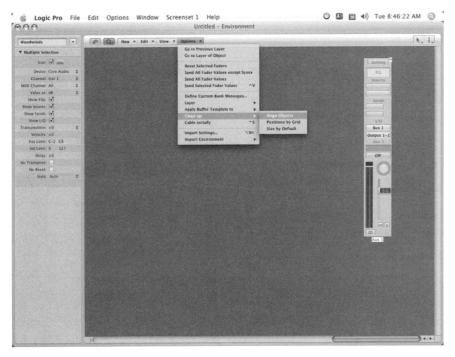

Figure 7.6   Cleaning up an Environment layer.

Figure 7.7   The Woodwinds Environment layer with the desired EXS24 instruments and an aux with Space Designer assigned to Bus 1.

Tutorial 8: Modifying Your Orchestral Template for Score Printout in Logic Pro 9

Is Logic Pro 9's Score Editor every bit as good for printing out parts and full scores for vocalists, instrumentalists, and conductors as dedicated score applications, such as Finale or Sibelius? No. Are they as good as sequencers as Logic Pro 9 is? No.

So if you are going to do work where you want it to sound great and then you want to print out parts for real players, is LP9 a very viable choice? Absolutely! I have prepared and printed the parts and scores for well over 200 TV episodes/films for myself and other composers.

The Score Editor is *very* deep, and there is no way I am going to teach you all there is to know about how to use it in this tutorial. The bible for Logic's Score Editor is still Johannes Prischl's *The Logic Notation Guide*. Although it was written years ago, so little has changed with Logic's Score Editor that it is still the best resource; see http://prischl.net/LNG.

Assigning Default Staff Styles for Regions

This is a very simple process, but a little time consuming if you have a lot of tracks.

1. Choose a track in your Arrange window. Make sure that the Region Parameter box is visible in the Inspector by opening the disclosure triangle if necessary.

2. At the bottom of the Region Parameter box, you will see Style: Auto, which means that Logic Pro is going to make an educated guess as to what staff style is required. See Figure 8.1.

Let's see how well Logic guesses.

1. Create a new empty project with one software instrument track. Use the Pencil tool to create a blank region at the beginning of the project.

2. Load in a flute patch. Open the Score Editor, and you can see that for an EXS24 instrument that I chose playing a flute patch, Logic has decided that a piano staff is appropriate, as shown in Figure 8.2. Wrong!

So much for that.

1. Close the Score Editor and delete the region.

2. With the Pencil tool, again create a blank region, and in the Region Parameter box, set the style to Treble.

3. Open the Score Editor, and now you see a treble clef, which is what a flautist reads. See Figure 8.3.

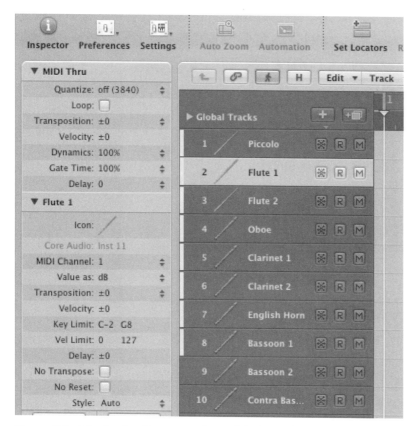

Figure 8.1   The Region Parameter box with the staff style assigned to Auto.

4.   Delete the region. Don't worry; the next time you record a region, the same staff style will apply.

Now you need to assign the staff styles for every other track in your Arrange window. You do not need to create regions for this, although many users prefer to have a blank region on each track, so that if you choose Delete Unused (Tracks), they will not be deleted.

Yes, this is a bit of a PITA and takes a little time, but once it is done and part of your template, you need not do it again.

Considerations

You need to make some decisions. Obviously, players who play transposing instruments need to have staff styles chosen for their parts that are transposed. In Figure 8.4 you can see a B♭ trumpet track properly assigned to a transposed staff style.

When you do the full score for the conductor, however, you need to decide whether you are going to print a concert (non-transposed) score or a transposed score, as Logic Pro 9 does not have the

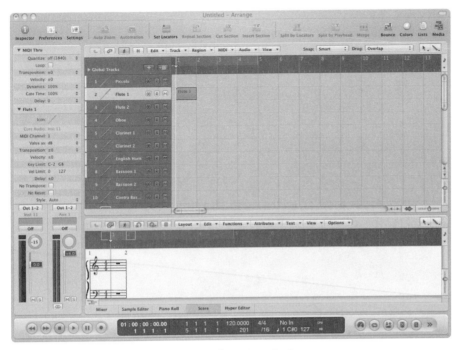

Figure 8.2   LP9's staff style selection when Auto is chosen.

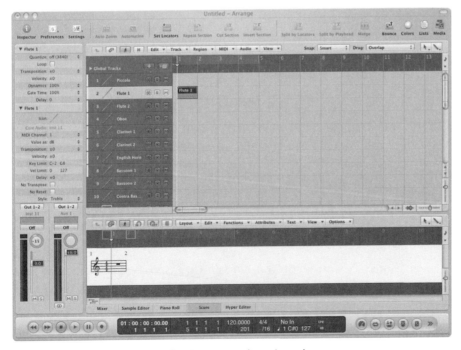

Figure 8.3   LP9's staff style selection properly assigned.

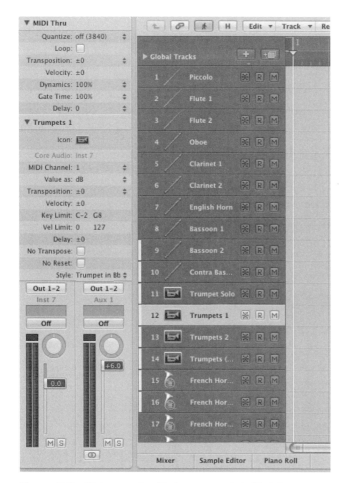

Figure 8.4   B♭ trumpet with transposed staff style.

ability to globally assign scores to print non-transposed (concert) but with transposed parts. When I was a Composition major at Boston Conservatory of Music, we mostly studied and wrote concert scores. When I did post-graduate study with the late and great Hollywood orchestrator Albert Harris, he advised me to get in the habit of reading and conducting from transposed scores, which I have done. Either way, if you are not the conductor/client, you need to know what they want, and if it is concert, before you print out the full scores you will need to reassign the staff styles to non-transposing ones.

There are users who have created templates with incredibly elaborate Environment tricks with meta event faders, transformers, and so on to make it possible to use one project for Logic's MIDI playback, parts printout, and score printout. Although I am not daunted by the complexities of the Logic Environment, when I look at these it makes my head hurt.

Personally, I have set my template for transposed parts, and after I have played in and edited all the parts and made them sound as I want, I then save the project under another name and make whatever adjustments I need, such as entering dynamics, slurs, articulations, and so on. And I print out the parts. Then I save it under another name and do the same for the full score.

Johannes Prischl is more of a one-project-for-all-purposes kind of guy, and in his book you will find some very clever tricks he employs to accomplish this.

Neither way is wrong; they are just different approaches. You can now delete the Undo History and save this as a template, and you are fine.

Let's take things a step further, however, and create some score sets for entering editing, dynamics, text, articulations, and so on.

1.   If you have not already done so, create a blank region on each track, as you see in Figure 8.5.

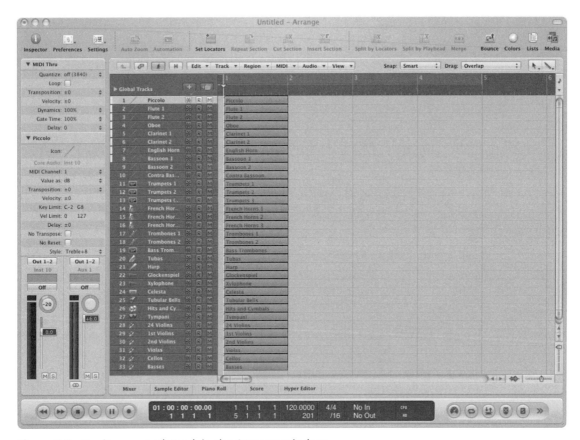

Figure 8.5   Regions on each track in the Arrange window.

2.   Under the large Logic Windows menu, choose Score. (The Score Editor that is part of the consolidated window is not well suited for this work IMHO, so consider creating a screenset with the Score Editor if you have not done so already.)

3. With no region selected in the Arrange area, make sure that the link is set to the Purple link, which is the full score hierarchy. In the upper-left corner, you will see that the Score Editor defaults to a score set called All Instruments, which is not editable. Use Command+A to select all the regions in the Score Editor.

4. From the Score Editor's Layout menu, choose Create Score Set from Selection, and LP9 will create an editable score set with a perfectly ridiculous name, which you will see where All Instruments was before.

5. Double-click on the name to see the contents and rename it perhaps, as in my example, Orchestra. See Figures 8.6 and 8.7.

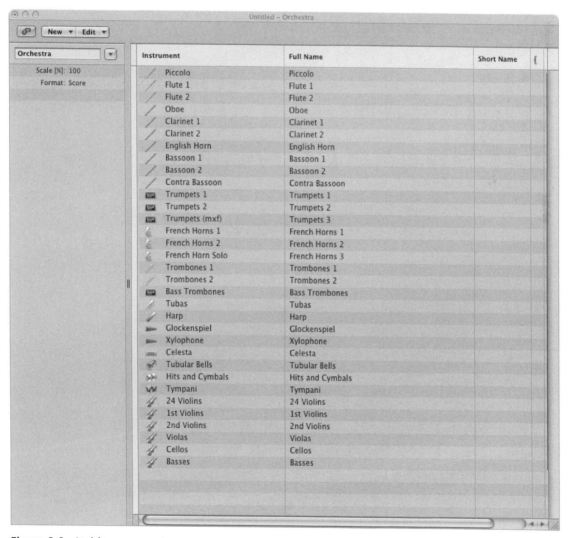

Figure 8.6   Inside a score set.

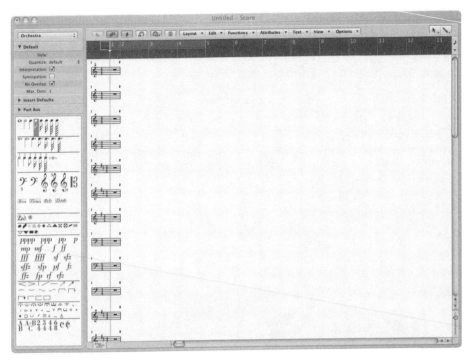

Figure 8.7   An orchestra score set.

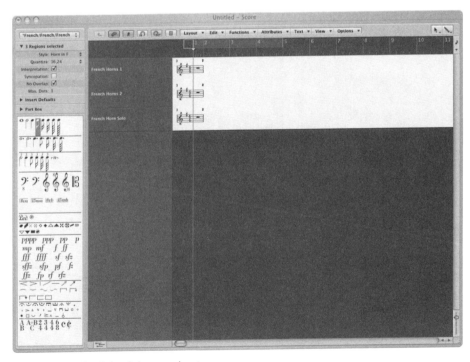

Figure 8.8   The French horn subset.

Let's create a subset for French horns only.

1. Return to the All Instruments score set.

2. Shift-select the three French Horn regions, and under Layout, choose Create Score Set from Selection. You now have a score set just for French horns. See Figure 8.8.

You can create as many of these in your template as you would like, and you can even import them from your template in another project.

Once again, delete the Undo History and save it as your orchestral template, overwriting the original, and you are good to go!

Becoming a Logic Pro 9 Stud: Techniques for Composing and Editing with Logic Pro 9

2

The tutorials in this chapter address issues and techniques in a Logic project to help composers, arrangers, and songwriters create mix-ready MIDI and audio parts.

Tutorial 9: Advanced Quantize Techniques for Natural-Sounding MIDI Parts in Logic Pro 9

In my journey as a Logic Certified Trainer, I have been surprised by how many otherwise quite knowledgeable users still rely on hard quantizing, which is snapping 100 percent to a predetermined grid. Although this might be a fine choice for musical genres such as techno or trance, it certainly is not for those who are trying to simulate live players with some of the many excellent software instruments and sample libraries.

Let's explore Logic Pro 9's many options in creating a natural-sounding piano part.

Hard Quantizing with the Region Parameter Box

Open a new project using an Empty Project template and add one software instrument.

1. Load in a piano channel strip. I am using Steinway Piano Studio, although you may use Ivory, Art Vista Virtual Grand, or any other third-party piano library you prefer.

2. Record an eight-bar MIDI region. Do not go to great lengths to play it particularly well, but also do not go to great lengths to play it badly.

3. Select the region in the Arrange area and look at the Region Parameter box where it says Quantize. I will assume that you are already familiar with choosing one of the preset quantize grids. Open an Event List Editor. See in Figure 9.1 the MIDI data of the region I recorded for this demonstration.

4. Play and listen. It does not sound very tight, and the data in the Event List shows why clearly.

5. In the Region Parameter box, select a quantize grid. In this example, choose 16th note. Now look at the Event List, and it is immediately evident that the notes have been

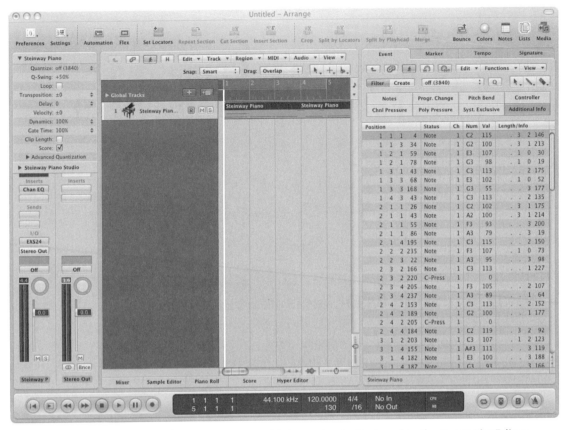

Figure 9.1   A MIDI region in the Arrange area with its contents displayed in the Event List Editor.

snapped to the grid 100 percent. When you now play it back, it sounds very rigid and un-musical, which is not what we are striving for.

The answer is to use the Advanced Quantization Parameters.

Using the Advanced Quantization Parameters for More Musical Quantization

Now we will explore all the possibilities for more musical quantization that the Advanced Quantization Parameters provide.

1. At the bottom of the Region Parameter box, you will find a disclosure triangle next to Advanced Quantization. Click the disclosure triangle, and the box magically transforms itself to display the Advanced Quantization Parameters. (Okay, so it isn't magic, it's code.) Alternatively, press Option+R, and it opens as a floating window that you can put anywhere on your screen(s).

2. Look halfway down the box and notice that you now have the following additional choices: Q-Swing, Q-Strength, Q-Range, Q-Flam, Q-Velocity, and Q-Length. See Figure 9.2.

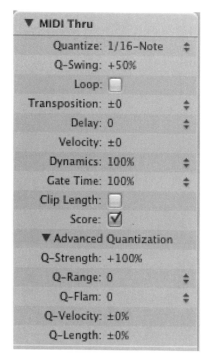

Figure 9.2   Advanced Quantization Parameters in the Region Parameter box.

Q-Flam

I will not be taking these options in order; I will take them in order of what I perceive to be of importance for this example. First up is Q-Flam. No matter how skilled a pianist you are, when you hit a bunch of notes with multiple fingers simultaneously, you do not hit them at the exact time, which is part of the reason why the hard quantizing we have done does not seem natural. Q-Flam allows you to preserve the natural differences in the simultaneous attack. Q-Velocity and Q-Length are only used in conjunction with groove templates, so I will not be discussing them in this tutorial.

1.   Next to the Q-Flam menu, where it presently displays 0, double-click and type 3. Look at the Event List and notice that in the places where simultaneous notes are struck, a separation of three ticks is preserved, as you can see in Figure 9.3.

2.   If you play it back and listen, it already sounds a little more musical. Next up is Q-Strength.

Q-Strength

1.   If you set Q-Strength to a value of 88 percent, you are essentially telling Logic Pro 8/9 that when it encounters notes that are not right on the grid, it should move them 88 percent of the way onto the grid. Next to the Q-Strength menu, where it currently says 100%, double-click and type in 88. Look at the Event List in Figure 9.4 and notice that the data is now considerably more varied.

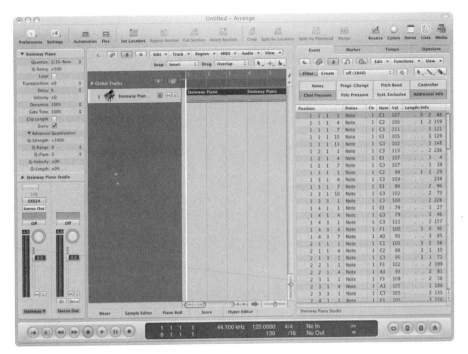

Figure 9.3   A MIDI region with a Q-Flam setting.

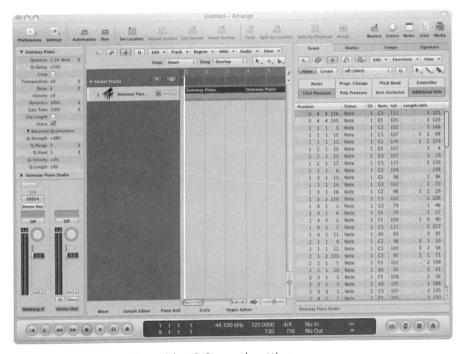

Figure 9.4   A MIDI region with a Q-Strength setting.

2. Play it back and listen. Now it sounds much more musical and yet still in time. In other words, it is starting to sound like a good pianist rather than a bad one or a machine, which is our goal. However, there is one problem. The first two notes are before the project beginning of 1 1 1 1, so we will not hear them.

3. Highlight the two notes and double-click. You may now simply type in 1 and hit Return, and the problem is solved.

But there is more to do. Let's explore Q-Range.

Q-Range

Q-Range now allows you to decide which notes are to be moved 88 percent onto the grid (in our example) and which are to be left where they are. With the default setting of 0, all the notes are moved onto the grid by the Q-Strength percentage. With a negative setting, only notes that are off the grid by more than the setting will be moved onto the grid, while those that are not as far off the grid will be left where they are. This is quite powerful and musical but is dependent on the part being reasonably well played to begin with. A positive setting leaves notes that are way off where they are and moves the ones that are closer to correct. I would probably only use this to preserve a drum fill. If it were a piano riff, I would simply de-quantize those notes.

1. Next to the Q-Range menu, where it currently displays 0, double-click and type in -20, or a 192nd note. Play and listen. It is sounding more human, which I like, but perhaps a little too sloppy. So now, because of the range setting, let's raise the Q-Strength to 90 percent.

2. Play and listen. Much better, but it feels just a little stiff. Although you are not playing a swing part, that does not mean it shouldn't swing a little. Q-Swing to the rescue!

Q-Swing

Q-Swing's percentage value alters the position of every second point in the grid, which gives it a swingier feel. The default of 50 percent does not alter the feel. More than 50 percent swings more, while less introduces a pre-delay, which sounds odd to my ears. We only need a subtle amount.

1. Next to the Q-Swing menu, where it currently displays 50%, double-click and type in 54%.

2. Play and listen. We are almost there.

3. The first note is three ticks early, so grab the first three notes and move them to 1 1 1 1. This preserves the distance of those notes in that chord.

4. Play and listen. Uh-oh, I played this a little too well!

5. Now change the Q-Range to -30 and the Q-Strength to 80%.

6. Play again and listen to what you now can see in Figure 9.5.

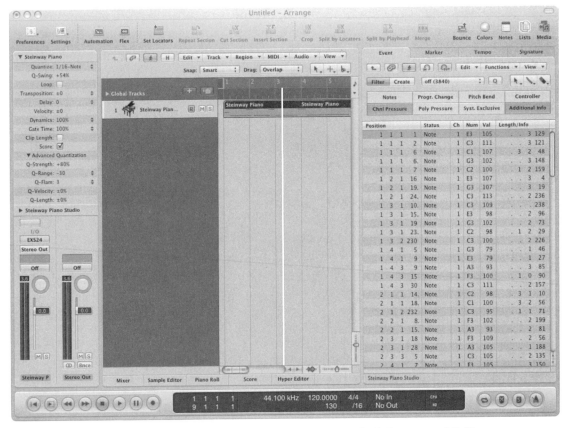

Figure 9.5   The MIDI region with settings for Q-Swing, Q-Strength, Q-Range, and Q-Flam.

I now have created a very musical and human-sounding piano part. Bear in mind that this is as much art as science, and the results you get using any combination of the Q settings with the Advanced Quantization Parameters will depend on the skill of the player, the desired degree of tightness, and, yes, taste.

Let's explore a little further. The piano part I created is a fairly common '60s pattern. I start with a Quantization setting of 1/16 note with a Q-Strength of 85%, a Q-Range of −30, and a Q-Swing of 54%, with no Q-Flam. I play it back, and it sounds pretty good but a little stiff. See the Event List in Figure 9.6.

I now adjust the Q-Range to −35 and bump up the Q-Swing to 56%, with no Q-Flam. I play it back, and it sounds better, but it's still not quite the feel I want. See Figure 9.7.

Hmmm, maybe the issue is the initial Quantize choice. I change it from 1/16 to 8 & 12, which tells Logic to round it to either the nearest eighth note or eighth note triplet, depending on which it is closer to. Just to see, I adds 3 ticks of Q-Flam. See Figure 9.8.

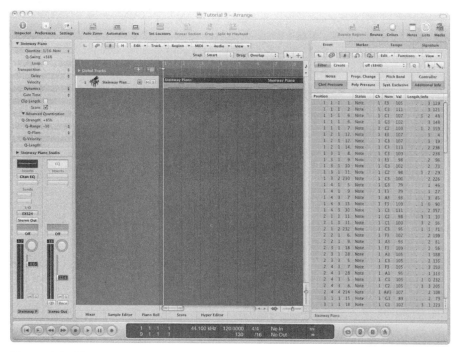

Figure 9.6   The MIDI region with more settings for Q-Swing, Q- Strength, and Q-Range.

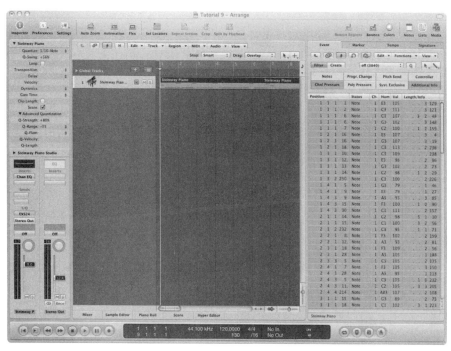

Figure 9.7   The MIDI region with more Q-Swing and more ticks in Q-Strength.

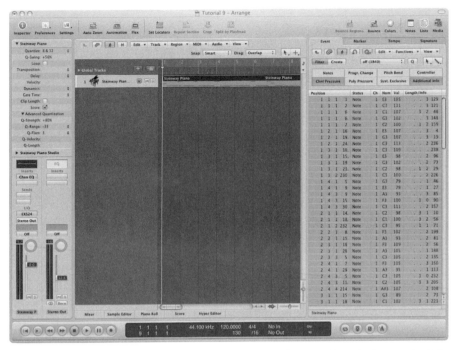

Figure 9.8   The MIDI region with adjusted settings for Q-Swing, Q- Strength, Q-Range, and Q-Flam.

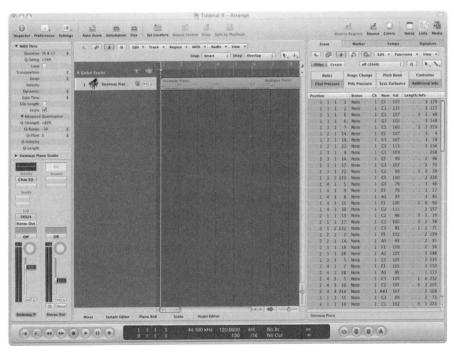

Figure 9.9   The MIDI region with my final settings for Q-Swing, Q-Strength, Q-Range, and Q-Flam.

Quantize	Q-Strength	Q-Range	Q-Swing	Q-Flam
1/16	85.00%	-30	54.00%	
1/16	80.00%	-35	56.00%	
8 & 12	80.00%	-35	56.00%	3
8 & 12	82.00%	-30	58.00%	3

Figure 9.10   The MIDI region with my final settings for Q-Swing, Q-Strength, Q-Range, and Q-Flam.

Almost there, but now it is a little too loosey-goosey. So now I will increase the Q-Strength to 82% and the Q-Range down to −30 ticks to tighten it up a little. I like it! See Figure 9.9.

Obviously, all of my choices are extremely arbitrary and dependent on the nature of the material, but hopefully this gives you a glimpse into my thought process as I approach this task. In Figure 9.10, you can see a little comparison chart of the settings I used.

Tutorial 10: Placing Regions Efficiently in Logic Pro 9

Logic Pro 9 has many ways to precisely place a region in the timeline of the Arrange area. As is true of many things in life (Jay waxes philosophically), there may be such a thing as too many choices. So I will try to whittle them down for you.

Using the Key Commands for Go to Position and Pickup Clock to Place Regions

This key command combo is the preferred method of the Apple Pro Training books, so we will explore this first.

1. Open a new empty project and create four stereo audio tracks with Open Library checked.

2. In the Library tab, navigate to the Loops tab.

3. One by one, carelessly drag four blue Apple Loops into the Arrange area.

4. Close the Media area.

5. Press Option+K to open your Key Commands window. I am using the standard U.S. with Numeric Keypad preset.

6. Search for the words Go to Position. While Apple has been known to change preassigned key commands in updates, as I write this it defaults to the forward slash next to the right Shift key in the standard set. You should see something like you see in Figure 10.1.

7. Now do the same for Pickup, which defaults to the semicolon in the standard set.

8. Close the Key Commands window.

9. Press the key command for Go to Position. Notice that there are fields for entering the playhead position in either bars/beats or SMPTE time. Enter a position.

10. Select one or more regions in the Arrange area and press the key command for Pickup Clock. Notice that the region moves to the desired timeline position.

This certainly works well, but it requires either using two key commands or manually moving the playhead and using the Pickup Clock key command. Either way, this is two or three steps, if you include selecting the region. That is one more step than I wish to have to do.

Using the Event Float to Place Regions

If you are like me, you already always have an Event Float as part of a locked screenset with an Arrange window. If not:

1. Under the Options menu or by using the Option+E key command, open an Event Float.

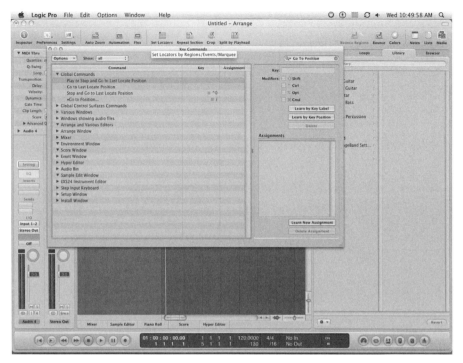

Figure 10.1   Finding Go to Position in the Key Commands window.

2. Place it where you want it on your screen and unlock and then relock your screenset (see Figure 10.2).

3. Highlight one or more regions, and in the Event Float you can type in a bar/beat position, and the regions will move to that position. If the regions are at different positions, rather than move them both to the same position, it will preserve the distance between them. If you click on the note symbol on the right-hand side of the Event Float, it will change to the entry fields for SMPTE position.

    See Figures 10.3 and 10.4 for before and after pictures.

This is now down to two steps, including selecting the regions. Much better!

Using the Event List to Place Regions

This is simply a variation on the Event Float technique. The advantage of using the Event List is that you see the big picture. This is my personal favorite.

1. In the Media area, open the Event List. Here you see all the regions. If you had MIDI regions as well as audio regions, and the Content Link (yellow) was enabled, you would

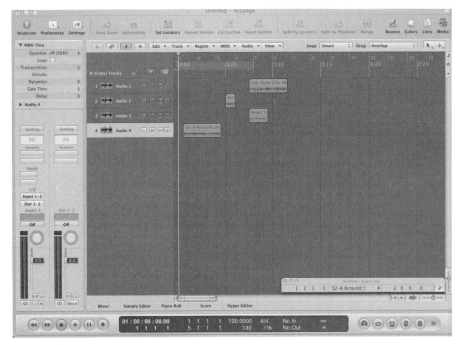

Figure 10.2   A locked screenset with the Event Float.

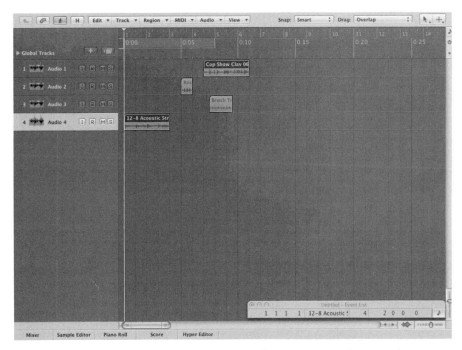

Figure 10.3   Highlighted regions' positions before moving with Event Float.

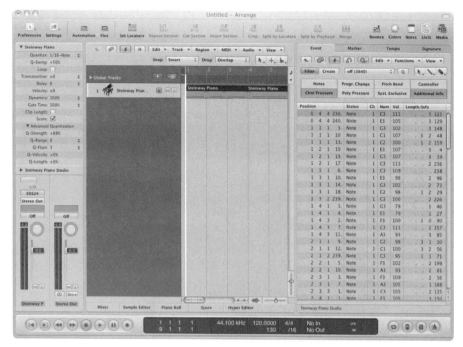

Figure 10.4 Highlighted regions' positions after moving with Event Float.

see the contents of the MIDI files, so you would want to change the link to the Same Level Link (violet).

2. Highlight one or more regions and double-click on one to type in a new position, and the regions will move to that position. Once again, if the regions are at different positions, rather than move them both to the same position, it will preserve the distance between them. Under the Event List's View menu, you can change the display to SMPTE positions. See Figures 10.5 and 10.6.

Here is another helpful tip: To change several regions to one position in one go, highlight the regions and, while holding down the Shift and Option keys, drag in the Position field to the bar/beat or SMPTE position you want, and all the selected regions will move to that position.

Figure 10.5   In the Event List's View menu, changing the display to SMPTE time.

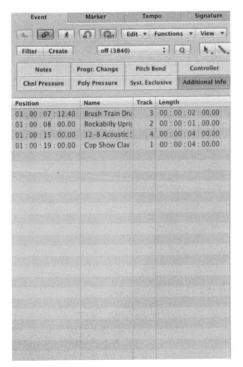

Figure 10.6   The Event List displaying regions in SMPTE values.

Tutorial 11: Using Groove Templates for an MPC3000-Like Feel

Many hip-hop music creators either have transitioned to Logic Pro from Akai hardware boxes, such as the MPC3000, or simply loved the feel of MIDI parts that were created with them. While they love the power of MIDI editing and all the software instruments and plug-ins that come in Logic Pro, they want that idiosyncratic, and frankly sloppy, MIDI swing timing that an MPC brings to the party.

With Logic Pro 9's ability to create groove templates, you can replicate these feels to a greater degree, utilizing some grooves that are available on the Internet, thanks to a source called Deep Blue Secret. Whoever this enterprising fellow is, he created a scale of MIDI notes and quantized them in the MPC3000. He then exported them as MIDI regions to Logic. Frankly, he has saved us a lot of time and trouble.

1. You will first need to download these by copying into your browser www.deepbluesecret.com/mpc.zip.

2. You will then have a Logic song named MPC_3000_Q.lso (Logic Pro 7 song) that you can open in Logic Pro 9. You should see two folders, one with sixteenth-note quantized regions and one with eighth-note quantized regions. See Figure 11.1.

Figure 11.1   The LP7 song with the MPC3000 quantized regions opened in LP9.

3.   Press Command+A to select them both and then Command+C to copy them.

4.   Close the project and open your template of choice. For this tutorial, let's open a new project and create two software instrument tracks.

5.   Press Command+V for paste, and you will see a dialog box appear. Choose Use the Selected and Following Tracks even if the track object types do not match. See Figure 11.2.

6.   Click OK. Right-click on Track 1 on the track header and reassign Track 1 to No Output.

Adding the MPC3000 Quantize Choices to Your Logic Template

These Quantize choices are project specific, rather than global in LP9, so it is wise to have them in a template.

1.   Double-click on the sixteenth-note folder, and it will open up. You will see 26 tracks with 26 regions, ranging from 50% swing, which is no swing at all, to 75% swing. Less than

Figure 11.2   The Paste dialog box.

50% would move the notes to the left on the grid, removing a swing feel, while 51% moves them 1% to the right, 52% moves them 2% to the right, and so on, adding more swing feel. Musically, moving to the left would not help you with the MPC-like feel, which is why the creator started with 50%, no doubt. See Figure 11.3.

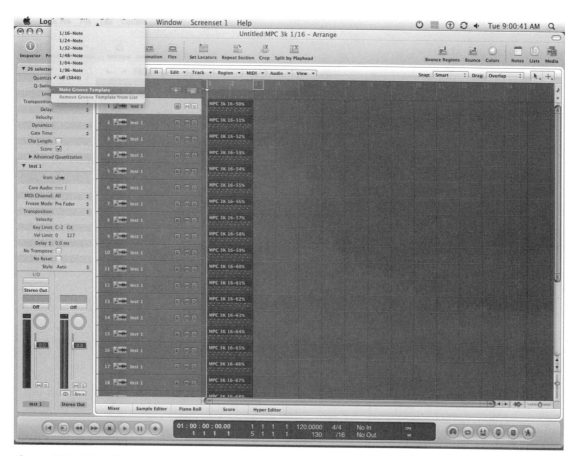

Figure 11.3 The sixteenth-note quantize grooves.

2.   Press Command+A to select them all.

3.   Under the Region Parameter box in the Inspector, navigate to the Quantize presets, and at the bottom you will find Make Groove Template, as you see in Figure 11.4.

4.   Double-click in the background of the Arrange area to return to the higher hierarchy, and the folders are viewable once again.

5.   Select the first track, and in the Inspector, click on the Quantize selector. Now you see all these MPC3000 sixteenth-note quantize choices, as shown in Figure 11.5.

Figure 11.4   Making the groove templates.

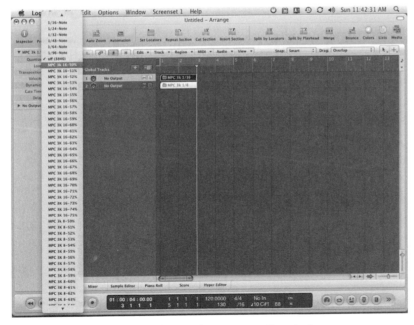

Figure 11.5   The MPC3000 sixteenth-note quantize choices.

6.   Open the eighth-note folder and repeat all the same steps. Now when you go to your quantize choices, you also see the MPC3000 eighth-note quantize choices, as shown in Figure 11.6.

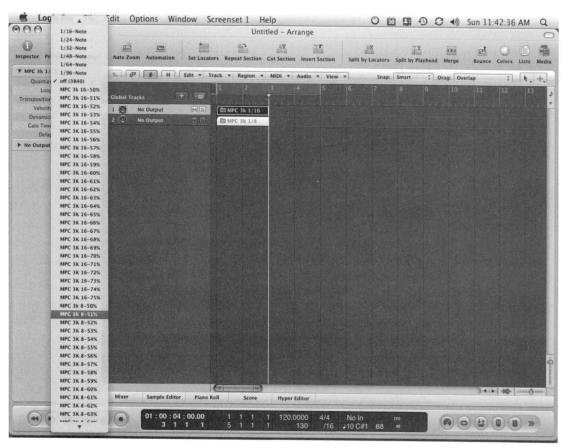

Figure 11.6   The MPC3000 eighth-note quantize choices.

Once again, it is very important to remember that these choices will only be available to you if the regions are saved as part of your template. You will, however, probably want to hide them. I will assume you know how to hide tracks, but if you do not, then consult the LP9 manual.

Now you can save or re-save your template with these MPC3000 quantize choices available to you.

Working with the MPC3000 Quantize Choices
Let's have some fun!

1. Open the Media area and choose the Loops tab.

2. Navigate to Drums > Acoustic and find the green Apple Loop named Bedrock Drumset 01, using a GarageBand drum kit.

3. Drag it to the Arrange area at Bar 1 and loop it. Play it back and listen. This is a pretty straightforward rock beat. Let's get funky!

4. In the Transport bar, double-click on the tempo and change it to 96.

5. In the Inspector, in the I/O on the fader, change the software instrument to Ultrabeat.

6. In UB's preset menu, navigate to Drum Kits > Hip Hop Sly Kit, as you see in Figure 11.7.

Figure 11.7   The Hip Hop Sly Kit preset in Ultrabeat.

7. Select the region, and in the Quantize menu, choose MPC 3K 8-65%. See Figure 11.8.

8. Play back and listen. Now it is a totally different thing!

Figure 11.8   The newly created MPC3000 quantize choices.

We're not finished yet!

1. In the Loop Browser, navigate to the Percussion loops and find Beachside Conga 02.

2. Drag it to the Arrange area at Bar 1 and loop it. Play it back and listen.

3. Select the region, and in the Quantize menu, choose MPC 3K 16-60%.

4. Play it back and listen.

These MPC3000 quantize choices that we now have with the newly created groove templates in our Logic Pro 9 templates can be the springboard for lots of creative ideas for later use in future projects. And of course, you can use these same techniques to create groove templates from MIDI regions you played yourself that have the unique personality that your own playing may impart.

Tutorial 12: Multi-Timbral Software Instruments versus Stereo Instances in Logic Pro 9

The preference for one or the other workflow is one of the most debated, sometimes heatedly, topics of discussion among Logic Pro users, particularly those who came to it from another DAW. There are arguments to be made for and against both, and in this tutorial I will explore them to help you arrive at your workflow choices. While to the best of my knowledge Apple has not made any public statements about their preference, I think the fact that the only truly multi-timbral software instrument that comes as part of Logic Pro is Ultrabeat, and particularly not the EXS24, speaks volumes. Personally, I sometimes use both, depending on the software instrument.

Advantages and Disadvantages of Each

Let's explore the CPU and RAM usage impact of each method.

1. Open a new project with four software instrument tracks, non-multi-timbral.

2. In the Transport, double-click where it says CPU to open the System Performance meter and lock the screenset. See Figure 12.1.

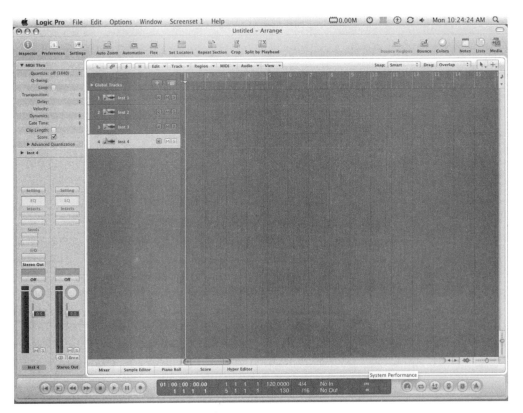

Figure 12.1   Opening the System Performance meter.

3. If it is not already in your Dock, go to the Utilities folder in your Applications folder and open Activity Monitor. Highlight Logic Pro, click the Inspect button, and click the Memory tab, as is reflected in Figure 12.2. If you are not using Snow Leopard (OS X 10.6) as your OS, it may look a little different. Note the Real Memory and Virtual Memory Settings and jot them down.

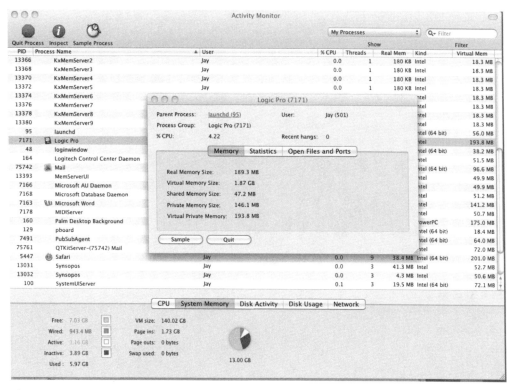

Figure 12.2 Activity Monitor inspecting Logic Pro's memory usage.

4. Back in Logic Pro 9, let us instantiate four powerful but CPU- and RAM-intensive software instruments. I will be using four stereo instances of Spectrasonics' Omnisphere. In the GUI's All category, I see a list of patches. For the sake of ease, I will load one of the first four patches in each of the Omnisphere instances. See Figure 12.3.

5. Arm them all and record a part and some simple volume automation with Logic's track-based automation, as you see in Figure 12.4.

The advantages to this workflow are immediately obvious to experienced Logic users. There is no conflict with the volume automation, where if you try to automate the region's MIDI channels discretely using Logic Pro's track-based automation, the software instrument itself would go cuckoo for Cocoa Puffs; there is no need to create auxes to have control over the audio level or to have discrete plug-ins. Look at the System Performance meter and notice that even on my now lowly quad-core Mac Pro, CPU usage is not a big deal.

Figure 12.3 Omnisphere's All menu.

So what is the downside? You cannot mix right inside the Omnisphere instance as you could if all four patches were loaded in the same instance, which some people prefer, but more importantly, let us return to the Activity Monitor and re-inspect Logic Pro. Notice that the Virtual Memory value with my usage has jumped to 3.00 GB. All 32-bit DAWs can only access up to 4 GB of virtual memory, and in the real world, when you hit 3.75, they start to get flaky.

Let us return to Logic Pro 9 and open a new empty project with one software instrument set to open multi-timbrally with four MIDI channels, as you see in Figure 12.5, closing the current one.

1.   Now instantiate an Omnisphere multi-output instance and, in the Mixer tab, load in those same first four patches from the All menu.

2.   Back in Activity Monitor, re-inspect Logic Pro. The Real and Virtual Memory usages both are down, in the case of the VM to 2.87. This may not seem like a big savings, but in a full project, it could perhaps make a critical difference. And if I wanted 8 Omnisphere patches, clearly the multi-timbral instance would be the necessary choice.

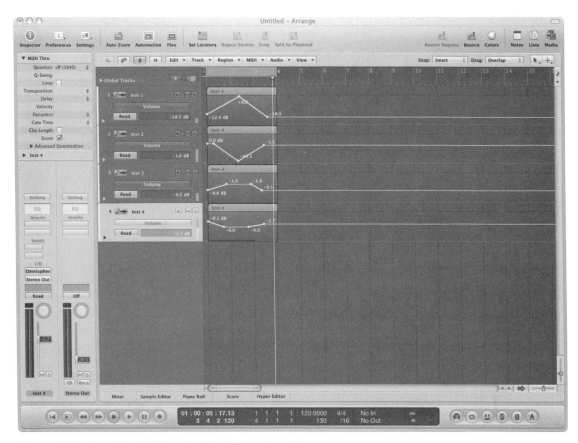

Figure 12.4   Four Omnisphere tracks with automation.

Figure 12.5   Creating a multi-timbral software instrument with four MIDI channels.

So what is the downside? To have discrete control of the audio, I must now create four auxes and assign them to receive four inputs from Omnisphere and assign the patches in Omnisphere to the corresponding outputs, as we did in Tutorial 2. Of course, I can just use a stereo instance and mix inside the Omnisphere GUI, but this limits my control.

But there are perhaps more important considerations.

1. As we did with the stereo instances in the first project, arm all the tracks and record a part.

2. Play back and notice the System Performance meter shows that it is all going to one core. Not good.

    (Of course, if I had four multi-timbral instances, they would theoretically spread to four cores.) See Figure 12.6.

Figure 12.6   The System Performance meter showing usage of one core by the multi-timbral Omnisphere.

3. Now try automating the MIDI channels, and as mentioned previously, Omnisphere itself goes wacky, sputtering and stuttering. Not good. Of course, there are ways around this problem, such as using cc11 (Expression) for volume with Logic's Hyper Draw and using the host automation as a kind of trim.

Considerations

So as you can see, it is not a clear-cut issue, and it depends on the nature of the software instruments itself. Some use more RAM and CPU merely by instantiating them than others. East West recommends using stereo instances in Logic Pro 9 rather than multi-timbral instances of libraries that use its Play engine. Eric Persing of Spectrasonics recommends some of each. These days, because Logic Pro and all but a couple of software instruments are not 64 bit, and this could change by the time this book has been released, I mostly use stereo instances in Logic Pro 9 and multi-timbral in a supplementary host, such as Vienna Ensemble Pro and Plogue Bidule. Unlike Logic Pro, these hosts *do* spread patches in a multi-timbral instance throughout the cores. I cover both of these applications in other tutorials in this book.

In conclusion, you can and should experiment with the software instruments you use most to achieve a balance of CPU and RAM distribution and the workflow you prefer.

Tutorial 13: Recording Two Different Software Instruments Discretely from Two MIDI Controllers with Logic Pro 9

My intention for this book was to choose topics that are either not explained or explained poorly in the manual and not covered in the Apple Pro Training series. Here I am making an exception, because for one reason or another many users seem to have trouble getting this to work properly, despite those resources.

Here is a typical scenario. I, a keyboard player, am working on a project in which I am playing software instruments from my keyboard controller. My friend, a terrific drummer, has kindly offered to bring over his V-Drums to record simultaneously with me. However, I do not want him to play a V-Drum kit. I want him to use my groovy Ultrabeat kit. (In the interest of full disclosure, as I write this I am not using V-Drums, but a little Boss drum machine as a stand-in.)

This should be a pretty straight-ahead affair, but like many things in Logic, it is perhaps not as intuitive as it should be.

Setting Up Logic Pro 9 and Your MIDI Controllers

1. Open a new empty project and create two stereo software instrument tracks, with Open Library checked.

2. Load 05 Keyboards > 01 Electric Pianos > Classic Wurlitzer 200a, or any keyboard sound, on Inst 1. In the Inspector, set it to receive on MIDI Channel 1. See Figure 13.1.

3. Load 04 Drums & Percussion > 03 Ultrabeat Drum Kits > Hip Hop Sly Kit, or any UB kit, on Inst 2. Close the Media area. In the Inspector, set it to receive on a different MIDI channel, perhaps MIDI Channel 10, which is the General MIDI default for drums.

4. Set your keyboard controller to transmit on MIDI Channel 1 and your drum controller to transmit on MIDI Channel 10.

5. Arm both software instrument tracks and play the keyboard controller and then the drum controller.

Wait a minute; they are both playing both sounds. That is *not* what we want. Here are the steps that people frequently miss.

1. Click the Settings button in the Toolbar and go to the Recording Settings. Halfway down in the dialog box is a section called MIDI. Check the box that says Auto Demix by Channel If Multitrack Recording, as you see in Figure 13.2.

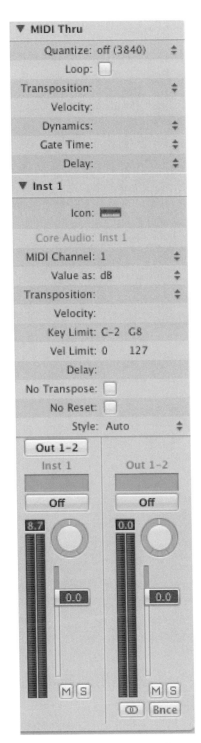

Figure 13.1   Inst 1 assigned to receive on MIDI Channel 1 in the Inspector.

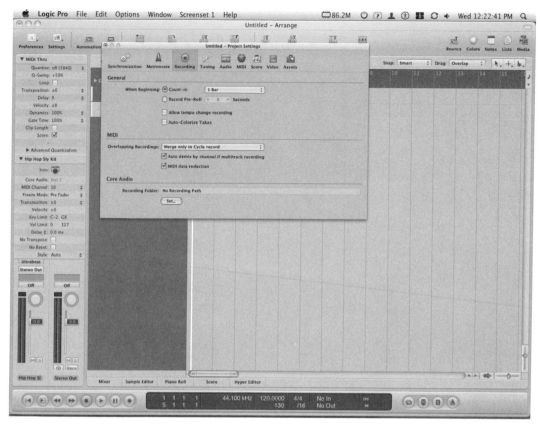

Figure 13.2   The Recording Project Settings with Auto Demix selected.

2.   Close the Project Settings.

3.   Play the keyboard controller and then the drum controller. Each is playing its intended software instrument discretely.

Now we're talking!

Recording the Two Software Instruments Discretely from the Two Controllers
This also tends to confuse users a little.

1.   With Inst 1 highlighted but with both software instrument tracks armed, go into record and play the two controllers.

2.   Uh-oh, it is only recording one region on the first track! Be patient, young Jedi, and keep playing.

3.   Hit Stop and notice that Logic now creates two regions, one on each software instrument track. But are they correct?

4.   Select the region on the first software instrument track and open the Event List. Notice that all the MIDI notes are assigned to Ch 1, and this is clearly the keyboard part. See Figure 13.3.

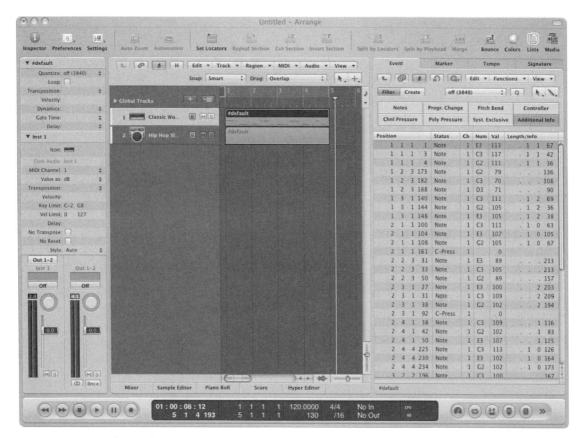

Figure 13.3   The first software instrument region in the Event List.

5.   Select the region on the second software instrument track, and in the Event List, notice that all the MIDI notes are assigned to Ch 10 and this is clearly the drum kit part. See Figure 13.4.

6.   Close the Event List and play, alternately soloing each.

You can continue to add players with other controllers playing other software instruments discretely. Indeed, you can have a whole virtual band!

Important Things to Remember

It is not uncommon for me to go to someone's studio and get this going for them, only to receive a frantic phone call or email from them several days later saying, "Hey, this was working when you

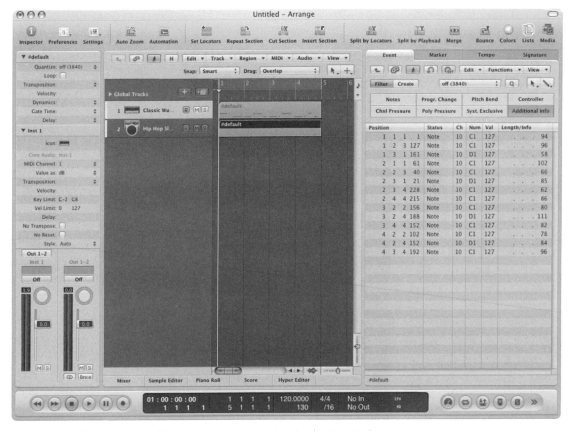

Figure 13.4   The second software instrument region in the Event List.

were here, but now my friend is over and we cannot get it to work." Here are a few important things to remember:

■   The Recording Project Setting for Auto Demix by Channel If Multitrack Recording is just that: a project setting, not a preference. Therefore it is not global, and it must be set up in each project in which you wish to enable it. I recommend you do this in your template(s), because there is no real downside to it that I can see.

■   The software instruments must be set up in the Inspector for the proper MIDI channels.

■   All the software instrument tracks must be armed in order to hear the controllers play discretely.

■   The controllers themselves must be set to transmit *only* on the proper MIDI channels. Frequently, the problem has been that the user is not familiar enough with how to do this in his or her controllers, because some of them, such as the V-Drums, have some challenging menus.

Tutorial 14: Creating a Tempo Map from an Audio File without Strong Transients

A few years ago, I was hired for a very unusual project. I was asked to take some classical pieces and add contemporary sounds to them. This meant I had to create a tempo map, because obviously these pieces were not recorded to a click. No problem, you say. Use Logic Pro 9's beat mapping global track to analyze the audio file's tempos and create a tempo map.

Well, this works well with audio files that have strong transients, but it does not work well with pieces of this nature. So what I needed to do was to create a MIDI guide track to beat map to. This is really a souped-up version of ReClock Song, which longtime Logic users will remember, but it works much better now.

The method I will demonstrate here will involve recording MIDI notes as guides to tell Logic where the beats fall. It is perhaps not as scientific as employing beat mapping in a more orthodox fashion, but I believe it can lead to some very musical results.

1. Open a new project with one software instrument track and one audio track.

2. Add your audio file to the project and drag it from the Audio Bin to the audio track in the Arrange area.

3. Instantiate an EXS24 drum kit on the software instrument track.

4. Under the Arrange window's local View menu, choose Configure Global Tracks for the tempo and beat mapping tracks.

5. Open the disclosure triangles, and you should now see something similar to Figure 14.1.

The next thing we need to do is determine the basic tempo. No problem; I will simply open the BPM Counter plug-in on the audio track and hit Play. And BPM tells me the tempo is . . . nothing. Once again, the lack of strong transients in this kind of piece has led us nowhere.

So now we need to get a little Old Skool.

1. Cycle the first four bars against Logic's metronome click.

2. Keep adjusting it until it sounds roughly correct—in my case, around 60 bpm.

3. Go to your Project Settings and check the Click While Recording and Only during Count-In options. See Figure 14.2.

Considerations before You Begin

Let's get to work.

1. The more familiar you are with the material, the better job you will do.

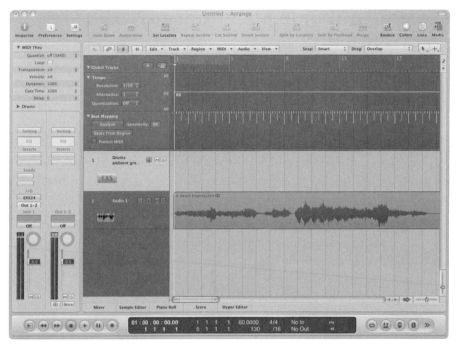

Figure 14.1   The Arrange window with the tempo and beat mapping global tracks.

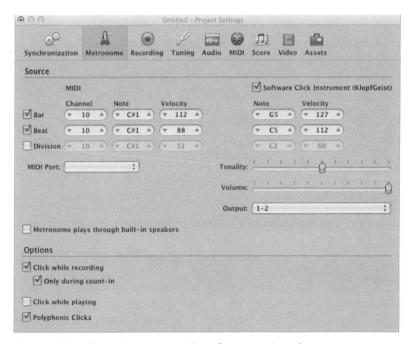

Figure 14.2   The metronome settings for count-in only.

2.　You might find it helpful to do this in smaller sections, rather than the whole song.

3.　Although you can use any sound, I like to use a side stick snare, which in most MIDI drum kits defaults to C#1.

4.　If necessary, make sure that you adjust the anchor precisely in the Sample Editor so that there is not blank audio at the beginning. (To do that, open the audio file in the Sample Editor, zoom in closely, and move the anchor so that it coincides exactly with the beginning of actual sound.)

Creating a MIDI Region to Beat Map To

1.　Arm the software instrument track and, after listening to the count-in, play the side stick snare. You should now see something like Figure 14.3.

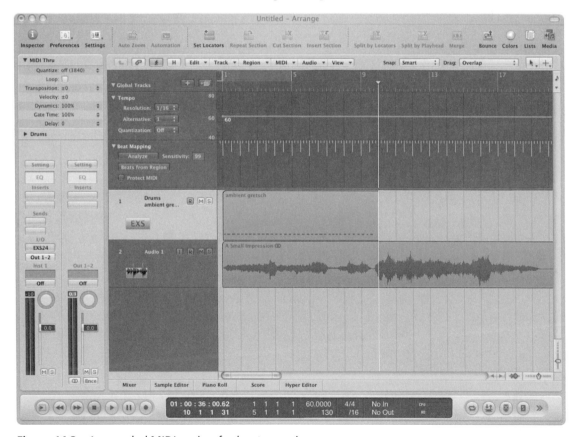

Figure 14.3　A recorded MIDI region for beat mapping.

2.　Highlight the MIDI region, and in the beat mapping track, click Beats from Region. A dialog box will pop up, and you can set the note value appropriately—in most cases, a 1/4 note, as shown in Figure 14.4.

Figure 14.4   The Set Beats by Guide Region(s) dialog box.

> You should now see tempo changes in the tempo track and mapped beats in the beat mapping track. See Figure 14.5.

Play and listen to the result. I did a pretty good job of playing against the audio, so depending on what parts I am going to add to this piece, I am perhaps done. If it is a drum loop, however, probably not.

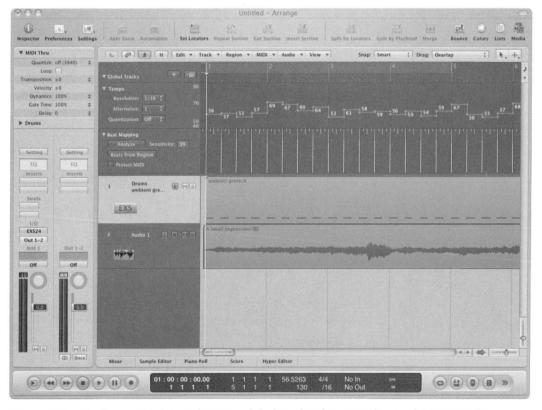

Figure 14.5   The beat mapping and tempo global tracks after mapping to the MIDI region.

In Figure 14.6, you can see that in my example the sustained chord that transitions from Bar 6 to Bar 7 is causing Bar 7's downbeat to hit a little early. I need to adjust this. (If you do not want to round off to round numbers, you need to hold down the Control key to bypass Logic Pro's Snap feature while you perform the next step.)

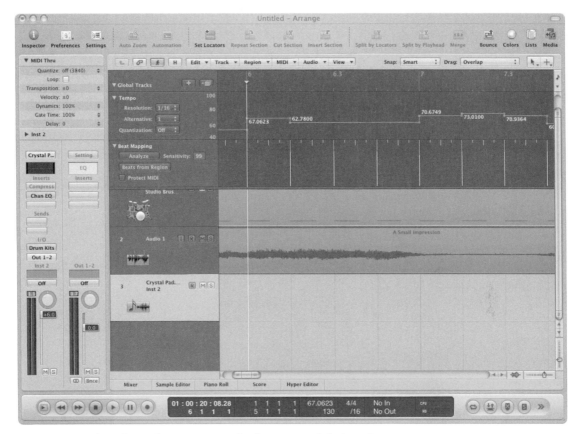

Figure 14.6 The adjusted tempo events in the tempo global track.

1. Double-click on the nodes on Beats 2, 3, and 4, and they disappear.

2. Use the mouse to drag the tempo event up to 62 bpm. Play and listen. The downbeat of Bar 7 is still a tad early.

3. Holding down the Control key, drag the mouse on the tempo until the number you see reads 62.7800. I play and listen, and it is perfect! See Figure 14.6.

You would now repeat these steps for the rest of the song if you were doing it in sections. At this point, you can mute, hide, or delete the MIDI region(s) and turn on the Logic metronome, and you have a click to play against.

An Optional Test for Fine Tuning

As I wrote earlier, how dead on this metronome click needs to be is dependent on the nature of what you are trying to accomplish. If you want to add pads, seeps, synthy beeps and boops, or FX, for instance, it probably can float a little. But what if you are going to add a loop that follows tempo?

1.   Open the Media area and select the Loops tab.

2.   Then navigate to All Drums > Acoustic > Lounge Jazz Drums 02, a green Apple Loop, and drag it into the Arrange area, below the track list. Logic creates a software instrument track for it with some plug-ins inserted. Play and listen.

Compositionally, what I have done is perhaps the worst idea of all time, but it alerts me to the fact that around Bar 2, Beat 4, my timing is not so hotsy-totsy and that I need to insert another tempo event to speed up a little.

1.   Double-click just above the line so that the cursor is the Pointer tool and a new tempo event is inserted.

2.   Set it to around 64.5000 bpm and play and listen. Much better!

I can now delete that dreadful loop and continue to work, confident in the knowledge that I am working to a tight tempo track.

Tutorial 15: The Power of Screensets

Longtime Logic users learned to use screensets to customize their workflow, but those who started with Logic Pro 8 and its "all in one" Arrange window may not be aware of just how really useful they are.

Screen real estate is a big deal with Logic Pro 9. Simply put, you want as much of it as you can have, either with a large monitor or with twin smaller monitors. If you have only a laptop, obviously you are limited, and the all-in-one Arrange window is good for you. Personally, I prefer twin monitors, and that is what you will see in this tutorial.

The Arrange window has some limitations. Notice that as you press the P key, the Piano Roll Editor opens. If you press the N key, the Score Editor opens, but the Piano Roll Editor closes. What if I want to see them both? Well, I have to open one or the other as a standalone window. What about the Event List Editor? I have to open Lists. What if I want to see different combinations of MIDI editors, the Mixer, different Mixer views, and so on? What if I want to see a great big bar display and a great big SMPTE display? I have to create them.

You get the point. Sometimes one size does not fit all. Let's get to work customizing screensets for a Logic Pro 9 template.

Creating a Locked Screenset

Let's create a screenset with an Arrange window with a giant bar display and a giant SMPTE display, and a Mixer window.

1. Open a Logic Pro 9 Empty Project template with just one software track, for now.

2. Open the Media area, navigate to the Loops tab, and choose a green Apple Loop. I am using 12 String Dream 01.

3. Drag it to the Inst 1 track Arrange area so what you now see appears similar to what you see in Figure 15.1.

4. Press Command+2 to open a standalone Mixer window. Drag it to the right side of your monitor (or in my case, a second monitor) and resize the Arrange window and the Mixer window so that it looks the way you want it to look. See Figure 15.2.

5. While holding the Control key, hold down the mouse in the black area of the Transport and navigate to Open Giant Bar Display, as you see in Figure 15.3.

6. Using the same method, open a giant SMPTE display. Resize and position them on your monitor(s) as you like. In my case, see Figure 15.4.

    Our next task is to lock the screenset so that it will always appear this way. This is very simple.

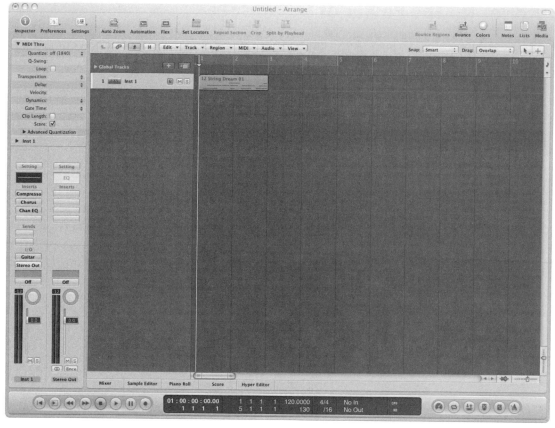

Figure 15.1   A green Apple Loop in the Arrange area.

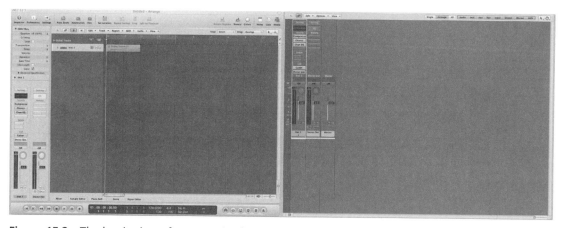

Figure 15.2   The beginning of a customized screenset.

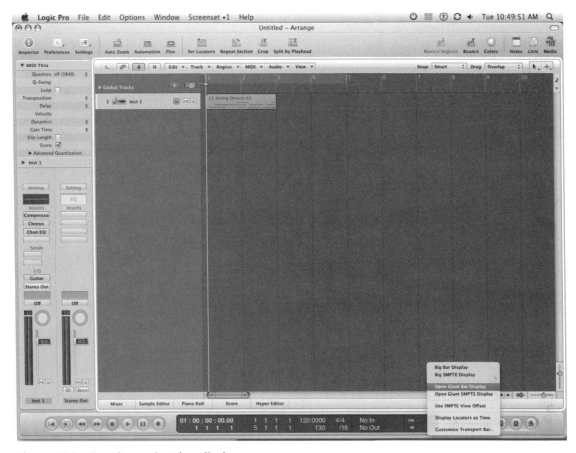

Figure 15.3   Opening a giant bar display.

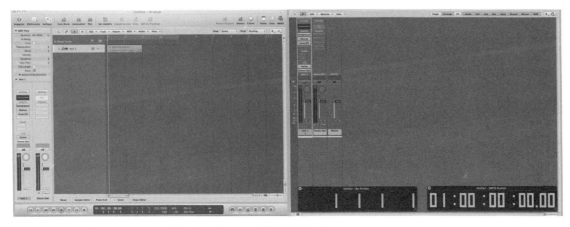

Figure 15.4   The screenset with giant bar and SMPTE displays.

7.   Under the Screenset menu, scroll down to Lock. (This can be assigned to a key command to toggle between the locked and unlocked states.) See Figure 15.5. A dot will appear just to the left of the screenset number—in this case, 1—telling you that you have a locked screenset.

Figure 15.5   Locking a screenset.

8.   Press 2 on your keypad and notice that it is the default screenset that we began with. Press 1, and you now see your customized screenset.

Let's create another!

1.   Press 2 on your keypad to open Screenset 2. If you try to close the Arrange window in this screenset, Logic Pro will think that you want to quit the project, so first you need to open another window.

2.   Press Command+6 to open a Piano Roll Editor and Command+0 to open an Event List.

3.   As before, resize and position the various editors to your liking on your monitor(s) and lock the screenset. In my example I have added a giant bar display and a giant SMPTE display and hidden the Transport and Inspector in the Arrange window, so that what you now see appears similar to what you see in Figure 15.6.

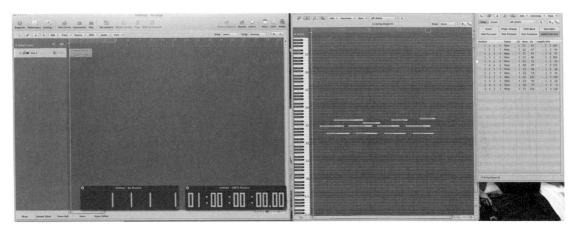

Figure 15.6   Screenset 2.

Hopefully, you now can begin to see how powerful a workflow tool this is. You can now toggle back and forth between the two simply by hitting numerical keys on your keypad. It is possible to create up to 90 of these babies (numbers 10, 20, 30, and so on are not available), but for most of us, nine or fewer is sufficient. In my template, in addition to the two I have created in this tutorial, I have a screenset with multiple Environment layers, another with two Mixers with one set to Arrange view and another set to Single view, a Score Editor combined with an Event List, and so on. (To access screensets 11–99, hold down the Control key and type in the numbers.)

You can even import them from your template or a saved project into another, which is really helpful when you are collaborating with another Logic user who may have different-size monitors and preferences for what he or she likes to see. Let's try it.

1.   Save this project either as a template or as a project. I am saving it to my desktop as Tutorial 15.

2.   Press Command+N to open a new empty project and close the present one.

3.   In the Toolbar, click Settings and navigate to Import Project Settings, as you see in Figure 15.7.

4.   Guide your mouse to the project with the screensets you wish to import and click on Import. A box will appear with a whole bunch of project settings you can import. Check Screensets. See Figure 15.8.

5.   Click on Import.

Figure 15.7   Import Project Settings from the Settings tab in the Toolbar.

Import Settings

☑ Screensets   ☐ Transform Sets   ☐ Hyper Sets

☐ Score Sets   ☐ Staff Styles   ☐ Text Styles
☐ Score Settings

☐ Sync Settings   ☐ Metronome Settings   ☐ Record Settings
☐ Tuning Settings   ☐ Audio Settings   ☐ Midi Settings
☐ Video Settings   ☐ Asset Settings

(Cancel)   (Import)

Figure 15.8   The Project Settings Import choices.

Voilà, it is done! You can now toggle between your customized, workflow-enhancing screensets simply by hitting numerical keys on your keypad.

Tutorial 16: Creating a Chord Chart with Logic Pro 9's Score Editor

My next book will probably be a book on preparing parts for sessions with Logic Pro 9's Score Editor. The only comprehensive book on the Score Editor is still Johannes Prischl's excellent book, *The Logic Notation Guide,* which was published in 1998. What is surprising (and disappointing) is how little real change has occurred to the Score Editor. What *has* changed for many users since that book was written is terminology and how we work. Many of us now use a lot of software instruments rather than hardware MIDI, and we address these in Logic directly, rather than using Logic's MIDI and multi instruments. Many others use a combination of both.

The Prischl book was intended to teach users everything there is to know about using Logic's Score Editor, from player-ready parts to engraved quality scores. However, today engraved scores are more likely to be done in applications designed primarily for score work, such as Finale or Sibelius. Logic is more likely to be used for printing out parts and scores for recording sessions, rehearsals, and so on with projects that were composed in Logic, and it is obviously an advantage to be able to stay in one application for the whole job.

Anyway, even users who are not likely to print up full concert scores sometimes need to print up a nice-looking chord chart, so that is what I will be teaching in this tutorial.

Entering and Editing Chord Text in a MIDI Region

1. Open a new empty project with one stereo software instrument track with Open Library checked.

2. Load 02 Acoustic Pianos > Pop Piano or any keyboard sound on Inst 1. In the Inspector, set it to receive on MIDI Channel 1.

3. Either play in or step enter in a piano part.

4. Under the Windows menu, open a standalone Score Editor. You will now see your region in the Score Editor. See Figure 16.1.

5. It defaulted to a Piano staff style, but we want a Lead Sheet staff style, which has already been created to use slashes for rests. So in the Region Parameter box in the Inspector, hold down the mouse on Style and switch from Piano to Lead Sheet. See Figure 16.2.

6. You may at this point wish to grab the region by the clef and drag it down a little and drag the line under the notes down a little to see the part better.

7. In the Part Box in the Inspector is a text icon that is a capital letter A. Click on it, and some text choices will appear. We will be using the one named Chord, as you can see selected in Figure 16.3.

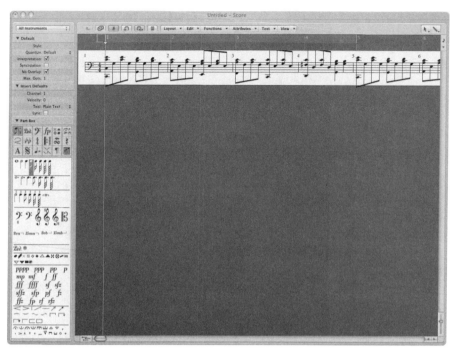

Figure 16.1   A MIDI region in the Score Editor.

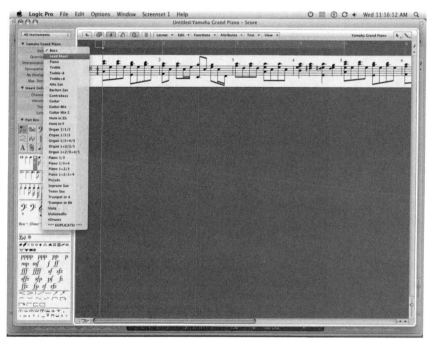

Figure 16.2   Choosing the Lead Sheet staff style.

Figure 16.3   Chord text chosen in the Part Box.

8.   Drag Chord to the beginning of the region right above the staff, and you will see a help tag appear that tells you what you are inserting and where you are inserting it. Make sure you are at the beginning. See Figure 16.4.

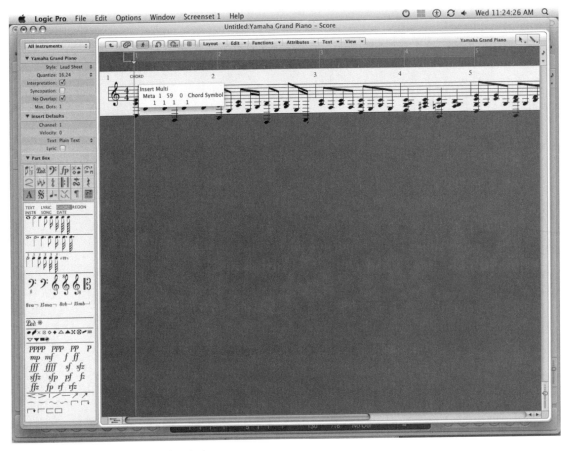

Figure 16.4   The chord insertion help tag.

9.   You will now see a blinking cursor at the insertion point. Type in a chord, and it will appear.

10.   Hit the Tab key on your keypad to advance to the notes where a chord change occurs and enter the next chord. Continue until you have finished. I have hidden the Inspector by pressing I on my keypad and zoomed in so you can see my whole region in Figure 16.5.

So far so good, but wait a minute—I see a mistake! At the downbeat of Bar 4, I entered a C7 sus instead of a D7 sus. Also, let's say that I want the word sus to come after the 7. I need to fix it.

1.   Double-click on the wrong chord, and a box will open that allows you to edit. Change the C to D.

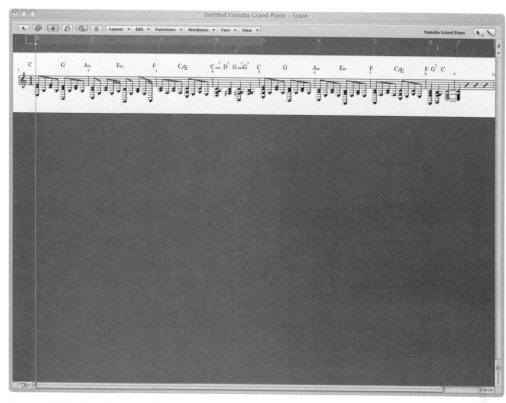

Figure 16.5   The Piano region with the chord changes entered.

2.   In the Root Note Extensions Upper field, delete the spaces before the 7.

3.   In the Root Note Extensions Lower field, add a space before the sus. It should now appear as it does in Figure 16.6.

Figure 16.6   Editing an inserted chord.

4. Click OK, and the chord will be changed.

None of these chord text events have any effect on the MIDI you have entered. They only are displayed.

Making the Score into a Chord Chart

Now it is time to turn this into a chord chart that all the rhythm players—in other words, keyboard, bass, guitar, and so on—can play from.

1. In the Region Parameter box in the Inspector, double-click on the Lead Sheet staff style, and it will open. See Figure 16.7.

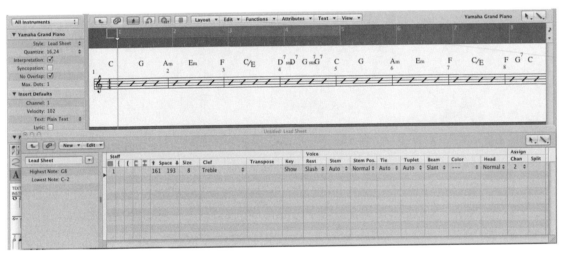

Figure 16.7   Editing the Lead Sheet staff style.

2. In the Assign column, notice that there is no MIDI channel assignment. Hold down the mouse and change it to anything but MIDI channel 1—in this example, MIDI channel 2. The notes are no longer displayed, only slashes.

   Fine, but what if I need some notes to be displayed to indicate rhythm?

3. Press Command+6 to open a Piano Roll Editor and position the Editors on the screen so that you can see them both. (This is where using screensets, as I discuss in another tutorial, is really handy.)

4. Select, for example, all the notes in Bar 1 in the Piano Roll Editor, and in the Inspector of the Score Editor, you will see they are all selected. You can now either leave the Piano Roll Editor open or simply close it.

5.   Where it says Channel 1, change it to Channel 2, and those notes will now be visible, as you see in Figure 16.8.

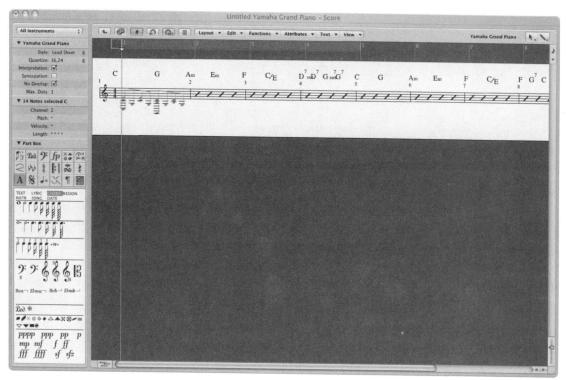

Figure 16.8   Notes are again visible in the score as the MIDI channel as been reassigned.

Okay, now I want to change them to only indicate rhythm.

6.   Shift-select the notes you do not need and delete them.

7.   Select the remaining notes and press Command+0 to open an Event List. The notes are highlighted here as well.

8.   While holding down the Shift and Option keys, drag the notes up to C4, and they now will all be C4s in the Score Editor. Delete any additional notes you want to or move them to indicate a different rhythm.

Let's change the note head so it will be clear this is for rhythm and we do not actually want that specific note played.

9.   In the Part Box's top row, click on the fourth box to the right to see our note head choices. I am going to use the second one.

10.   With the notes still highlighted, hold down the Shift key and drag the note head onto the first note. A help tag again appears to guide you.

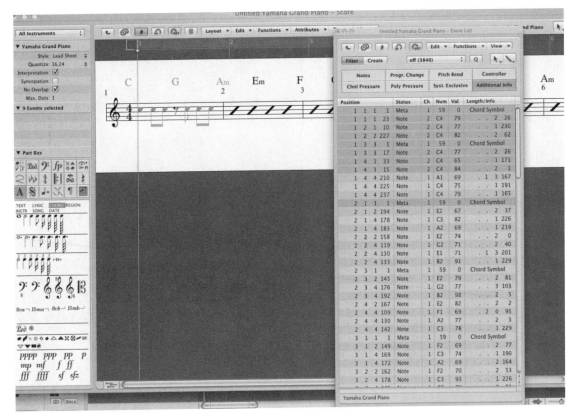

Figure 16.9   Notes displayed for rhythm.

11.   Great, they are all changed...except the first one. This bug has been around forever. Without holding down the Shift key, drag the note head onto the first note. See Figure 16.10.

Let's add a dynamic, make a meter change, and put in a double bar symbol to mark the end of the chart.

12.   In the Part Box's top row, click on the third box to the right to see our dynamics choices. I am going to use the default of mf (mezzo-forte) and simply drag it to 1 1 1 1 with the aid of the help tag.

13.   In my example, Bar 8 is clearly a bar of 2/4. In the Part Box's second row, click on the third box to the right to see our meter choices. I am going to choose 2/4 and drag it to Bar 8 with the aid of the help tag, and then 4/4 to Bar 9.

14.   Click the next box to the right, choose the double bar symbol, and drag it to the end. See Figure 16.11.

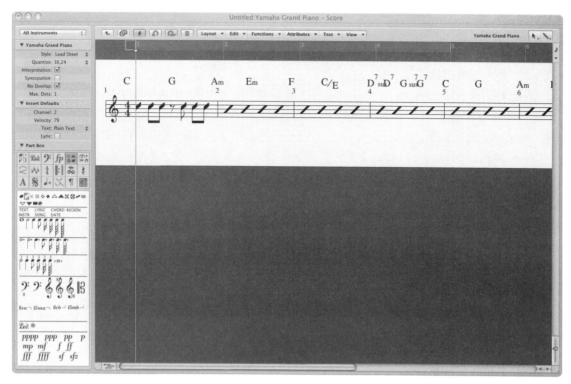

Figure 16.10   The notes with new note heads.

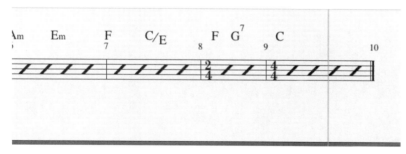

Figure 16.11   The end of the region with meter changes and a double bar symbol.

Meter changes and the double bar symbol are among a group of items that are global, affecting all parts in a project.

Preparing the Chord Chart for Printing

Let's make this more pro-looking. Most of what follows is subjective.

1. Under the local View menu, choose Page View. Also under View > Page Display Options, make sure Print View and Show Margins are selected. See Figure 16.12.

2. Under the local Layout menu, open Numbers & Names.

3. In the Bar Numbers section, I change the Vertical Position to a negative number, such as −6, change the Step to 4, and change Start With to 1.

4. I then uncheck Instrument Names, so that it now looks like Figure 16.13, and I close the Numbers & Names panel.

5. It now appears as in Figure 16.14. Better, but a little too crowded in Bar 4, perhaps. I can fix that.

6. I reassign the Command tool to the Layout tool. See Figure 16.15.

7. Holding down the Command key, I use the Layout tool to create a little more space between the chord changes, so it now appears as you see in Figure 16.16. This does not change its MIDI position, only how it looks.

8. I now hold the Command key and with the Layout tool, I grab Bar 8 and drag it down so that the last two bars are on a new line. See Figure 16.17. In many cases, this will help a lot, but in this case it was better before, so I press Command+Z to undo it.

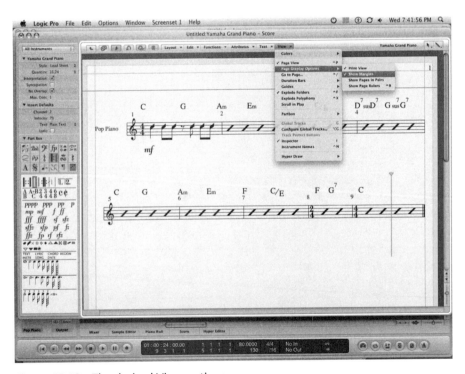

Figure 16.12   The desired View options.

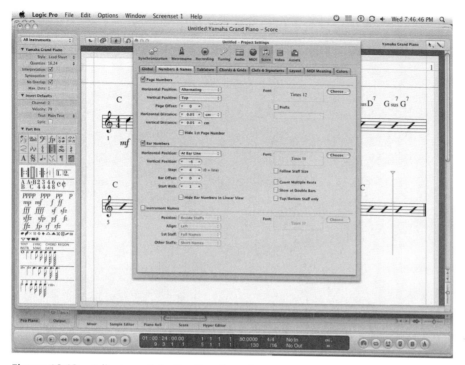

Figure 16.13   Adjustments in the Numbers & Names panel.

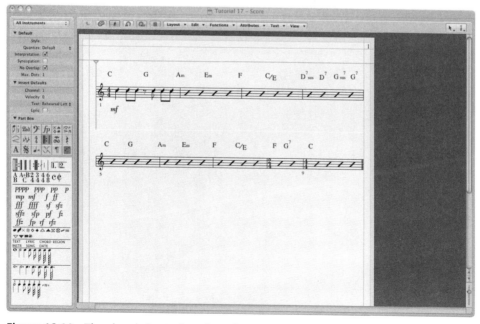

Figure 16.14   The chord chart after the adjustments.

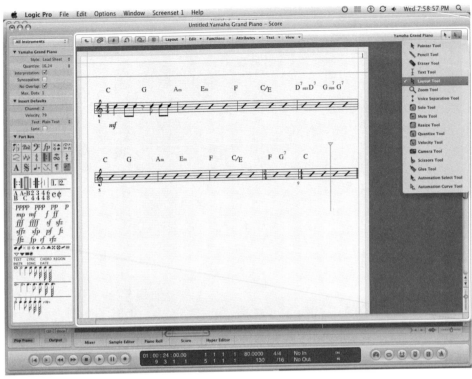

Figure 16.15   Assigning the Command tool to the Layout tool.

Figure 16.16   Using the Layout tool to space the chord changes.

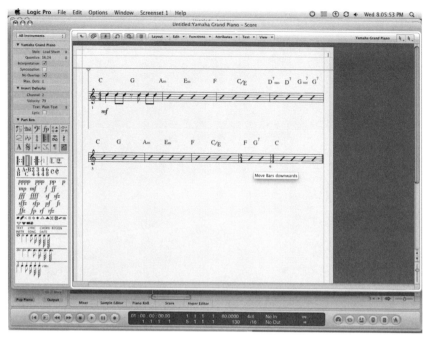

Figure 16.17   Using the Layout tool to drag the last two bars to a new line.

All that remains is to create some text styles for a title, instrument, tempo, rehearsal letters, and some directions, and then enter them. Once again, my choices are subjective.

1. Under the local Text menu, choose Text Styles and expand the window by dragging on the lower-right corner so that you can see the default text styles. See Figure 16.18.

2. Under the New menu in this window, choose New Text Style five times to create five new text styles (duh!).

3. One by one, double-click on them and rename them.

4. In the Example column is the font choice. They all default to Times, regular, size 12. Double-click on each one and reassign to taste. I am making the title Times, bold, size 18; the instrument Times bold 14; the tempo Times italic 14; the rehearsal letter Times regular 14, boxed; and the direction Times italic 14. All this is clearly evident in the Text Styles window, which you can now close. See Figure 16.19.

5. Reassign the Command tool to the Text tool and at the beginning of Bar 1, hold the mouse down just under the header area margins and, watching the help tag, drag straight up into the header. See Figure 16.20.

6. Release the mouse button and type in the title.

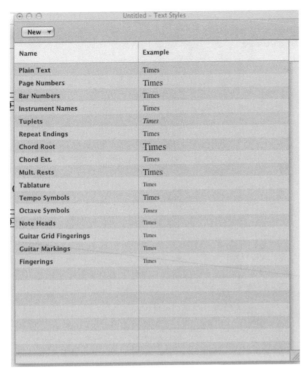

Figure 16.18   The Text Styles window.

Figure 16.19   The Text Styles window with the newly created text styles.

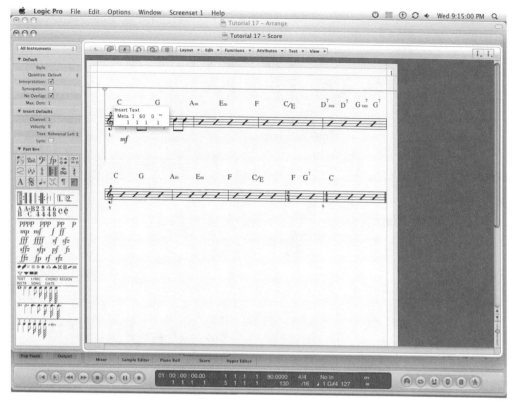

Figure 16.20   Dragging text with the Text tool into the header.

7.   With the text still highlighted, notice that in the text box in the Inspector, it is assigned to a Plain Text style, aligned left. Change it to Title, aligned center. In my case I entered it a little too high, so I adjust my Vertical Position, which was −45, to −80. See Figure 16.21.

Figure 16.21   Reassigning the text style, the text's alignment, and vertical position.

8.   Using the same procedure, I then enter an instrument name and tempo. Then, just under the header, I add a rehearsal letter. Finally, under Bar 2, I add a direction. It now appears as you see in Figure 16.22.

Our chord chart is now completed and ready to be printed!

Figure 16.22 The completed chord chart.

Tutorial 17: Plotting Hits in Logic Pro 9

A *hit,* or *hit point,* as the term is commonly used by those of us who write music for films and television, is a musical event that is timed to coincide with a moment in the picture to accentuate it and add to its impact, or more subtly, to subconsciously call attention to it so that future events will have been foreshadowed. Over the years, film scorers have accomplished this in a number of different ways.

- Conducting freely to picture, using streamers for the hit points. This takes a lot of skill.

- Conducting to a variable click track, created by plotting the hits with a calculator, or a book such as the *Carroll Knudsen Click Track Book* (discontinued), or a software program such as Opcode's Cue (sadly discontinued and missed).

- Finally, using Richard and Ron Grant's Auricle, a DOS-based program for PCs, which could also output streamers as well as variable clicks.

More and more, however, composers do it right in their DAW. Sometimes these events occur on scene cuts. Logic Pro 9 has a terrific ability to detect scene cuts and automatically create scene markers, which then can be beat mapped to create a variable-tempo click track.

The basic process of detecting cuts and creating movie scene markers is very well described in the manual and quite easy to understand. What I am going to do is propose a couple of extra steps to that technique and then approach the task from a different perspective.

Converting Scene Markers to Standard Markers and Moving Them a Few Frames

It is one of the peculiarities of the human brain that if you have a musical event coincide with a frame with a picture event, the brain will perceive the music as early. Composers, therefore, tried to make their musical events hit a little late, up to six frames. The music video era has accustomed viewers to quicker edits, so from two to six frames is what I now generally try for.

Unfortunately, detected scene markers are not editable, so you need to convert them to standard markers to move them.

1. In Figure 17.1, you can see a Marker List that shows detected scene markers that presumably I have beat mapped and created the necessary tempo changes. Under View, I have chosen Event Position and Length in SMPTE Units.

2. Select all by pressing Command+A.

3. Under the Options menu, choose Convert to Standard Marker. Notice that the little frame icon to the left of the marker name has disappeared. See Figure 17.2.

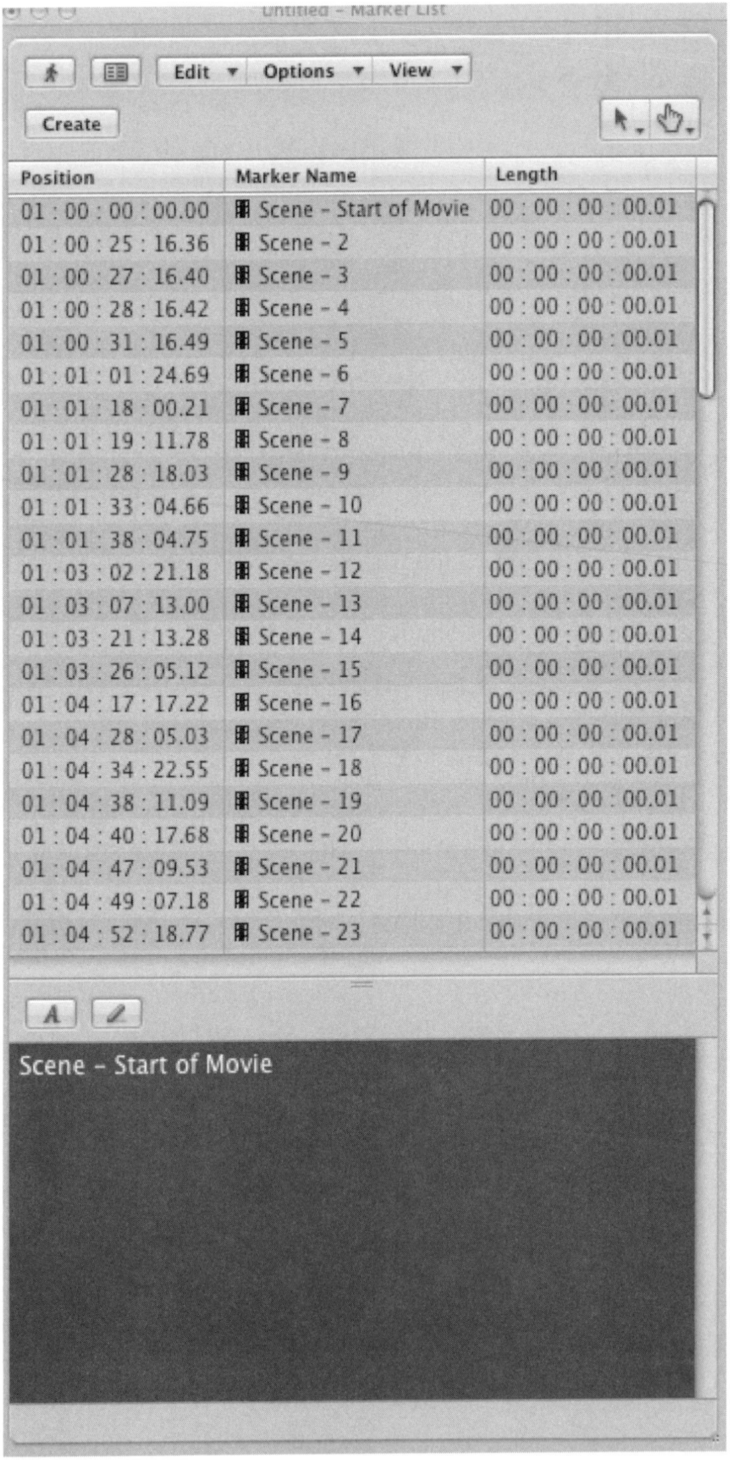

Figure 17.1 A Marker List with detected scene markers.

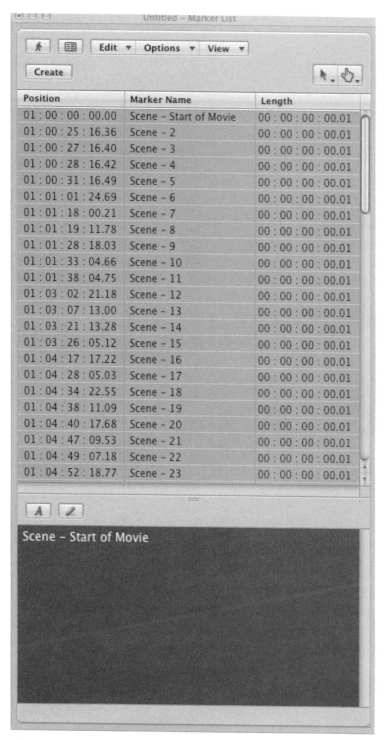

Figure 17.2   A Marker List with standard markers.

4. Now I can move the markers back a few frames so it looks best to my eye and rename them. I can also delete the ones I do not need, so I have a list that appears as in Figure 17.3.

Jay's Fly-by-the-Seat-of-Your-Pants Method for Plotting Hits

For me this is a more emotionally satisfying way of creating my tempo map for hits. The screenshots are from a film I co-composed with Adam Malamut, called *Nanny Insanity*, now available on DVD from Amazon. (Yes, I know, this is shamefully blatant self-promotion.)

This is not an actual cue I scored, but a "let's pretend" second cue in the second reel.

The first thing I do is play a piano part to develop my thematic material and find a tempo that works overall. Once I am locked into that and am totally familiar with the scene, I start to plot my hits. I am assuming that you do not have the luxury of having had a music editor give you the timings of where all the important picture events take place. This used to be common practice, but nowadays composers seem to be expected to do it all, so typically I will have spotted the cue entry and exit times with the director (film) or producer (TV) and maybe a couple of picture events that he or she deems important. Otherwise, I am on my own.

As you can see in Figure 17.4, I am starting this cue—let's call it 2m2—at a SMPTE start of 02:02:58:02 with a basic tempo of 114 bpm. I have adjusted the Movie Start time in the Video Settings in the Project Settings box so that the BITC (*burned in time code*) reads the same as the SMPTE time in my cue. I have decided that there are four hits I am going to try to nail in this cue. You can do this exercise without video simply by setting up the make-believe cue as I have. (For these timings, you need not worry about subframes, and you can turn them off in your Preferences if you want.)

1. Create a software instrument track and open an EXS24. You can either load a sound or leave it blank so it plays a sine wave.

2. Create a blank MIDI region with the Pencil tool and extend it to the length of the song, either by dragging it or adjusting it in an Event Float.

3. Open a view of the MIDI region in the MIDI editor of your choice. In my case, it is the Score Editor. Toggle the MIDI In button so it turns red. See Figure 17.5.

4. My first hit is at 02:03:08:06. Use your Go to Position box and type that into the SMPTE field, as you see in Figure 17.6. Play a note on your MIDI controller. (You can also do this with Logic's Step Input Keyboard.)

5. My second hit is at 02:03:35:00. Use your Go to Position box and type that into the SMPTE field. Play a note on your MIDI controller.

6. My third hit is at 02:04:25:03. Use your Go to Position box and type that into the SMPTE field. Play a note on your MIDI controller.

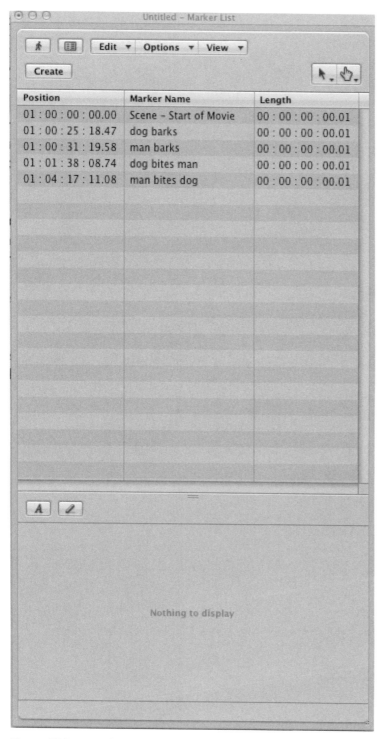

Figure 17.3   An edited Marker List.

Figure 17.4   The settings for the cue.

7.   My final hit, where the music will tail to the end, is at 02:04:33:01. Use your Go to Position box and type that into the SMPTE field. Play a note on your MIDI controller.

Close the Score Editor and open the Event List. None of these notes hit on the downbeat, although the first one hits pretty much on Beat 3 of the fifth bar. Now we have some decisions to make. Can I change the tempo and still have it work musically for me? Can I insert some meter changes and still have it work musically for me? Which hits are *really* important?

As I now reflect on some of my earlier scores, I went to too great a length to hit some things that were not that important, to the detriment of the music. It is a balancing act. Contemporary taste is not to hit as many things in a cue because it now appears cartoonish. (Obviously, if this were a cartoon, then we would have a lot of events to hit.)

Now, we have to experiment.

1.   In the Event List, select all, and under the Functions menu or by key command, choose Lock SMPTE Position. See Figure 17.7.

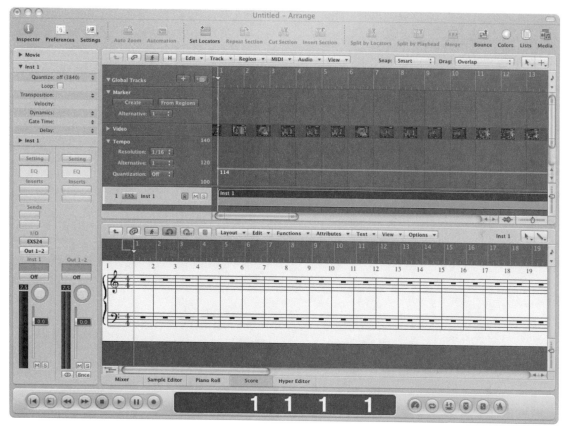

Figure 17.5 The Score Editor with MIDI In toggled on.

2.   If I decide that the first hit is indeed important and that musically I can live with it being a bar of 2/4 going into 4/4 at Bar 2, then the hit lands on the downbeat of Bar 6. Try this by typing in 2/4 in the tempo field of the Transport bar at the beginning of the cue. Advance the playhead to Bar 2 and type in 4/4.

Figure 17.6 The first hit entered in the SMPTE field of the Go to Position dialog box.

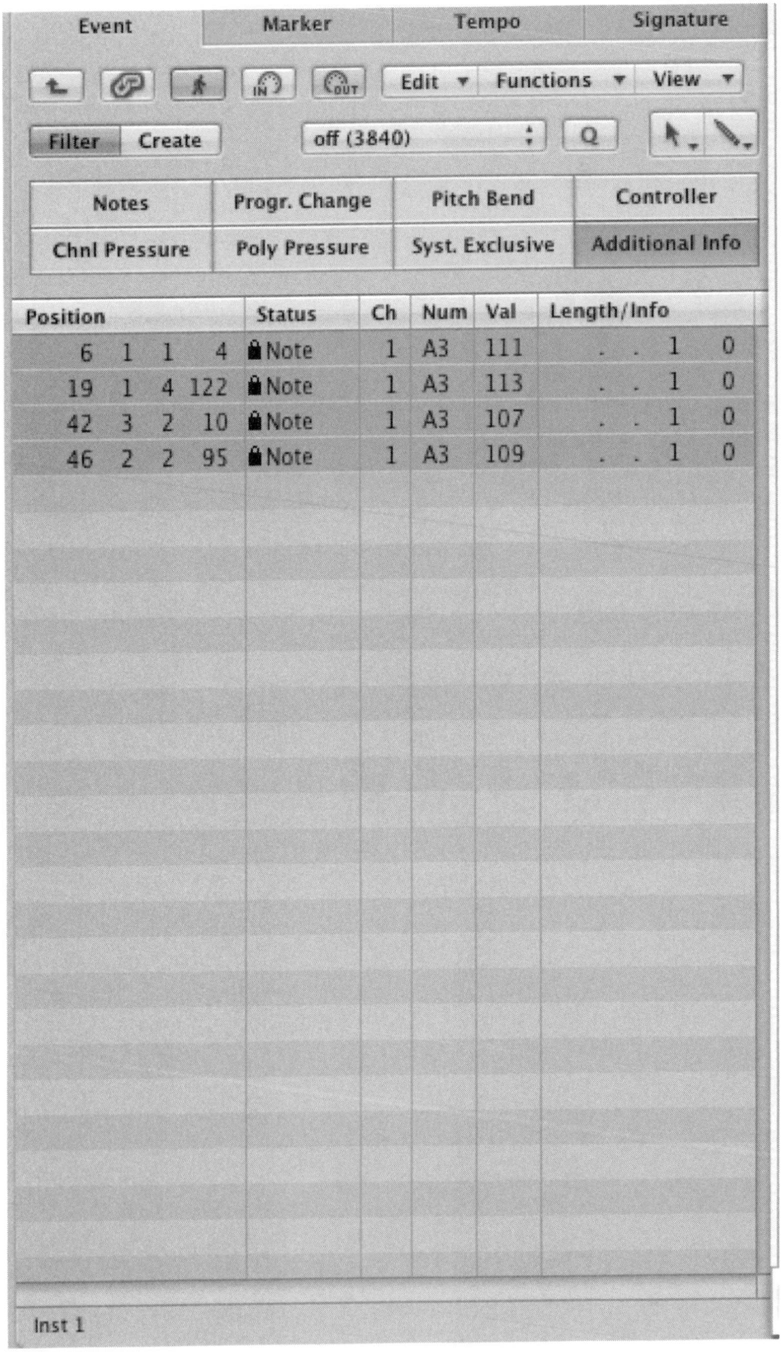
Event
Marker
Tempo
Signature
Edit
Functions
View
Filter
Create
off (3840)
Q
Notes
Progr. Change
Pitch Bend
Controller
Chnl Pressure
Poly Pressure
Syst. Exclusive
Additional Info
Position
Status
Ch
Num
Val
Length/Info
6 1 1 4 Note 1 A3 111 . . 1 0
19 1 4 122 Note 1 A3 113 . . 1 0
42 3 2 10 Note 1 A3 107 . . 1 0
46 2 2 95 Note 1 A3 109 . . 1 0
Inst 1

Figure 17.7 Notes in the Event List locked to SMPTE.

3. The next hit is early, but maybe some subtle tempo changes could make it land right. Navigate to Options > Tempo > Open Tempo List.

4. Under the Tempo List's Option menu, choose Tempo Operations. Let's get creative.

5. The scene gets more and more exciting, so I do not mind if the tempo picks up a little musically. By typing in the various fields, tell Logic to create some tempo events from Bar 2 to Bar 42 at a 1/8 density from 114 to 118 bpm, with Continue with New Tempo checked. See Figure 17.8. Click the Apply button.

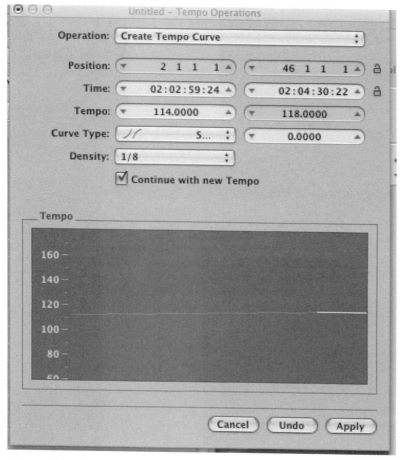

Figure 17.8   The Tempo Operations dialog box.

6. The second and third hits are off, but the fourth hit, which is the most important, is just a little early. Undo, then try the same thing using a destination tempo of 117.500. Not quite. Undo.

7. After trial and error, I find that 117.450 gets my last hit only 74 ticks late. I wonder how that translates into frames?

8.   In the Event List, under View, choose Event Position and Length in SMPTE Units to see that the fourth hit is only a single frame later than I spotted it. I can live with that.

You will find that through experience, you gain a sense of just how much you need to tweak the tempo events for your hits.

Considerations

At this point, you can go into the Tempo List and alter or delete some events and see how it affects your hits, but I suggest you flesh out your cue musically before you do too much of this.

This cue turned out to be quite difficult, didn't it? It will not always be so. Frequently, good film editors seem to cut to a beat, and once you find the correct starting tempo, a lot of hits just seem to fall into place. When they do not, sometimes you have to let go of some of the hits, as we did here. Sometimes if the hits are really important, you need to find a different starting tempo and musical concept. It is a craft that is as much art as science.

3

Getting in Touch with Your Inner Geek: Techniques for Recording and Mixing with Logic Pro 9

I f you are primarily a composer, songwriter, or musician as I am, the skills that engineers possess may seem quite alien. In this era of smaller budgets, we are frequently called upon to be ready to do it all. This chapter is geared toward helping budding engineers or even experienced engineers who may be new to Logic Pro 9 in these tasks.

Tutorial 18: Side Chaining in Logic Pro 9

A side chain is simply an auxiliary audio input to a synthesizer or effects processor. In this tutorial we will use side chaining techniques to apply vocoder effects to an audio file with the Evoc 20 PS and use side chaining for "ducking" a synth bass with a kick drum.

Adding Vocoder FX to a Vocal with the Evoc 20 Polysynth and Side Chaining

The vocoder has been and remains a popular element in contemporary music. Logic Pro comes with a quite nice vocoder software instrument, the Evoc 20 Polysynth. While it has the ability to be used as you would any software instrument and to play some effected vocal-ish sounds, its most popular use is a way of effecting recorded vocals while playing MIDI notes. You achieve this by utilizing the Evoc 20 PS's ability to side chain.

You can do this with any recorded vocal, but for the purposes of this tutorial, we will use an Apple Loop.

1. Open an empty project and create one stereo audio track and one software instrument track.

2. In the Media area, click the Loops tab and find the Vocals group of Apple Loops. You might have to click and hold on the double arrow in the lower-right to find it. See Figure 18.1.

3. Choose a loop such as African Mist Voice 01 and drag it onto the audio track at the beginning of the project. Close the Media area.

4. Hit Play and listen to it. It's quite nice, but not what we want.

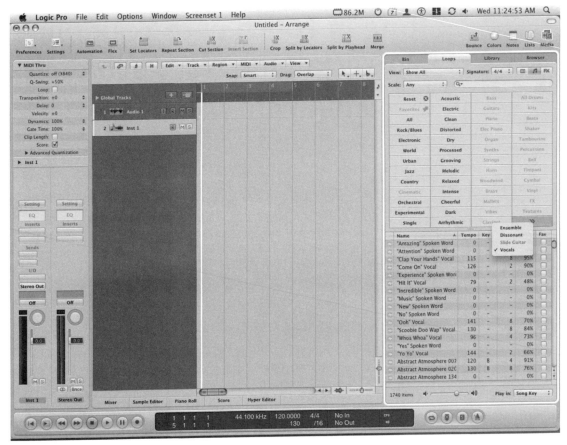

Figure 18.1   Finding the vocal loops in the Loops tab of the Media area.

5.   Create a four-bar cycle and listen to it until you are very familiar with it, particularly the rhythm.

6.   On the software instrument track, open the Evoc 20 PS.

7.   In the Synthesizer bank of presets, choose Alien Abduction (see Figure 18.2). Play and listen. Again, it is nice, but what we want to do is to effect the vocal loop with the Evoc 20 PS by playing MIDI.

8.   Notice that in the upper-right of the GUI, around the 2 o'clock position, the Signal is set to Syn, telling us that it is meant to be played as a synthesizer rather than effecting another track.

9.   In the Evoc 20 PS, load from the Vintage Vocoder bank, Electrified Vocoder. Notice that it defaults in the Signal area to Voc, telling us that it is meant for the purpose we want.

10.   Play and listen, and you hear nothing.

Figure 18.2   The Evoc 20 PS's Synthesizer presets bank.

11.   Change it to Syn and play and listen, and now you hear sound.

12.   Change the signal back to Voc.

13.   In the upper-right of the GUI, where you see Side Chain, set it to Track 1, Audio 1, as you see in Figure 18.3.

Here is where the fun begins!

1.   Hit Play and hold down a chord and listen. You hear a mixture of the original loop and the vocoder effect.

2.   While still cycling, try raising and lowering the faders on both the audio track and the Evoc 20 PS track to try different blends of the original loop and the vocoder effect.

3.   Experiment by playing quarter notes instead of a chord.

4.   Change the tempo.

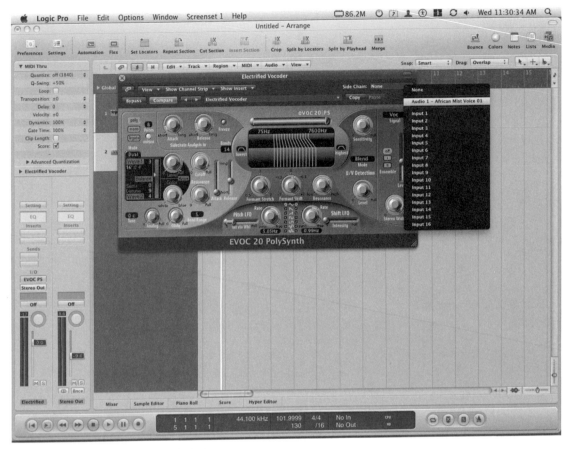

Figure 18.3 Setting the Side Chain input.

5.   If you only want the vocoder sound, in the Inspector assign the output of the audio track to No Output, as you see in Figure 18.4.

6.   Determine the notes you want to play and record onto the Evoc 20 PS track.

Now you have it. You can also employ similar side chaining techniques with the ES1, Sculpture, and—to a lesser degree, as it is only for modulation purposes—the ES2 and the EXS24.

Side Chaining Compressors

Perhaps the most common use of side chaining is with compressors. A popular technique is to use this for "ducking" a bass track with a kick drum.

1.   Create another software instrument track and instantiate an ES1.

2.   Click on the Media area and then choose the Library tab, which now will show you ES1-related channel strips. Choose in the 03 Synth Bass presets the one entitled Sequencer Bass. See Figure 18.5.

Figure 18.4   The audio track assigned to No Output.

3. In the first insert, load in Logic's Compressor plug-in.

4. Play and notice that the channel strip now goes way into the red, so turn down the gain until it does not.

5. Record the bass playing whole notes.

6. Create another software instrument and open an EXS24. Load in a drum kit, such as Big Beat Remix.

7. If you can, play in a simple kick drum part or step enter it. I am doing quarter notes.

Now we need to create an aux to use a bus to communicate between the EXS24's kick drum and the ES1's compressor.

1. With the Mixer open to Arrange view, click on the + sign to create an aux. Assign its input to Bus 1, as you see in Figure 18.6.

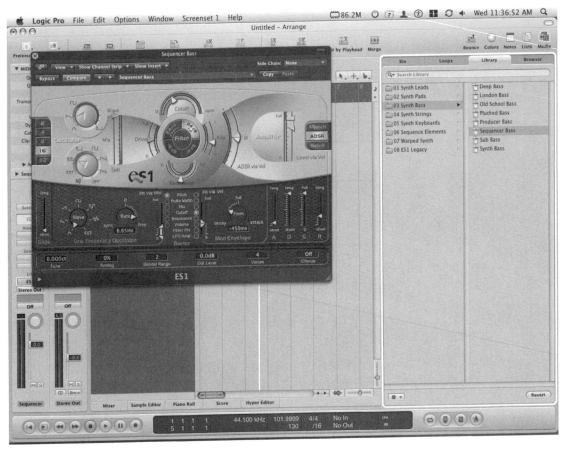

Figure 18.5   Choosing the Sequencer Bass channel strip.

Figure 18.6   The auxiliary channel strip creation dialog box.

2. On the EXS24 track, assign the first send to Bus 1 and adjust the level so that it is coming up strongly on the aux.

3. Open the GUI of the ES1 track's compressor.

4. Way down at the bottom of the list in the Compressor Tools bank called VCA Tight, assign the side chain input to Bus 1, as you see in Figure 18.7.

Figure 18.7   The Compressor's VCA Tight preset with the side chain set to Bus 1.

5. Play and listen. As it is playing, try making the attack and release quicker.

6. Drag the Compressor threshold way down so it kicks in at low level.

7. Drag the Gain fader up and down and notice that as the level of the compressor's output changes, so does the level you hear of the bass as it is side chaining through the compressor.

8. Raise the amount of signal being sent from the ES1 track to Bus 1, and now the kick sounds louder.

Try other presets and sounds. The possibilities with side chaining are endless!

Tutorial 19: Wise Gain Structure Techniques for Mixing In The Box within Logic Pro 9

This is perhaps the only tutorial in this book that will be deemed controversial. Indeed, there will be those who will say that I am full of what makes the grass green and who will tell you all the mathematical reasons why. And yet, over the years, I have eventually brought some of them at least partially over to my reasoning.

Let us start with the areas that I believe almost all experienced users will agree on.

■ In most genres of contemporary music, while analog distortion and anomalies can be deemed aesthetically pleasing, digital distortion is not. It is unpleasant noise and should be avoided.

■ Even in floatingpoint apps, such as Logic Pro and Digital Performer, much as it was/is in the case of tape recorders, it is very important not to clip (go into the red) the outputs used for bouncing, although it is less critical for individual channels due to the large amount of headroom built into floating-point applications.

Here is where opinions about how to deal with gain structure diverge. There are those who will tell you that since in Logic Pro 9 it does not matter if every single channel is wildly in the red as long as the outputs are not being clipped, all you have to do is lower the fader on the output until it is no longer in the red. They will further maintain that if you control the channels' levels by controlling the output internally in the GUIs of software instruments and FX plug-ins and raise the output so that the result is exactly at the same level, the bounces created will be exactly the same, and that is true.

I could almost buy this laissez-faire approach if one was using only Logic plug-ins, but most users are also using third-party software instruments and plug-ins, and while they must conform to the AU spec, we really do not know how they are processing internally.

It is also true that there could be distortion occurring within these plug-ins that Pre Fader Metering would not tip you off to, as it happens before it gets to the end of the signal chain in the channel strip. While that is no doubt true, it is also true that if you hear distortion that is coming from an undetermined source, channel strips whose level is going wildly into the red are probably a good place to start checking it out.

My experience has led me to conclude that even though Logic Pro 9 "is" a floating-point app and therefore is not distorting channels when it is shown in the red with Pre Fader Metering (more about this a little later in the tutorial), it is wise to stick to the traditional mix practices of analog tape/console and fixed-point apps and control the levels of what is going through the channel strip at their sources. I am convinced that this practice results in more open, better-sounding mixes. And as Paul Frindle, the creator of the Sonnox (formerly known as Sony Oxford) plug-ins, wrote in a discussion of this issue, "If I am wrong about this, where is the downside?" At the very least, you will be quite focused on every channel in your mix.

Pre Fader Metering

If you are recording a singer or a musician to a tape recorder, with a microphone or line out going into a console channel on most consoles, you adjust the level from the mic pre, amplifier, D/I box, and so on, and the meter on the console reflects the incoming level. If you pull down the fader's channel, you will hear the sound play back more softly, but the level you see on the meter will not change because it is showing you the level before the fader adjusts it. This is what is truly hitting the channel and is therefore, IMHO, the truth.

In my opinion, this is what you should replicate in your In The Box workflow, no matter what DAW you use, at least until your levels are set.

Let's set Logic's Pre Fader Metering to on.

1. Open a new project with four software instrument tracks created.

2. Holding down the Control key, click in the black area of the Transport and select Customize Transport Bar, as shown in Figure 19.1.

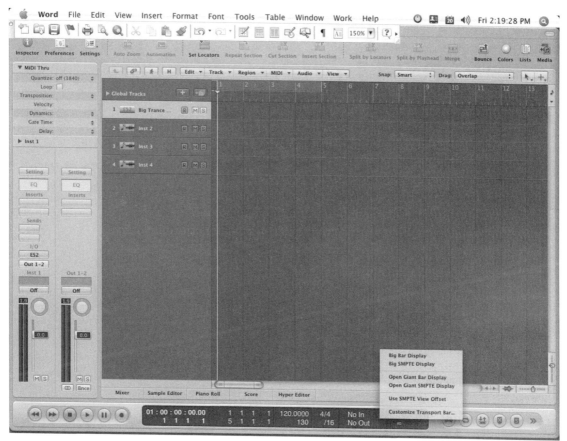

Figure 19.1   Customize Transport Bar.

3. Under Modes and Functions, check Pre Fader Metering. This creates a Transport button where you can toggle Pre Fader Metering on and off. See Figure 19.2.

Figure 19.2   A Transport with an enabled Pre Fader Metering button.

4. Click on the button to turn it on.

This is a project setting rather than a preference, so you will want to save this in your templates in order to keep it as a default.

Let's demonstrate exactly what we are talking about here.

1. On the first software instrument track, instantiate an ES2.

2. Click on the Media area and then choose the Library tab, which now will show you ES2-related channel strips. In the Warped Synth presets, choose the one entitled Metaloid.

3. Toggle off Pre Fader Metering. Play A3 on your keyboard hard and hold it down or use your sustain pedal. Notice it goes way into the red.

4. While continuing to hold the note, in the Inspector pull down the fader on the ES2 channel strip and notice that it gets softer and the level displayed lowers. Release the note and click on the clip meter to reset it.

5. Toggle on Pre Fader Metering. Play A3 on your keyboard hard and hold it down or use your sustain pedal. Notice it again goes way into the red.

6. While continuing to hold the note, in the Inspector pull down the fader on the ES2 channel strip and notice that it gets softer and the level displayed stays the same, showing you the level that is actually hitting the channel. Release the note and click on the clip meter to reset it.

Now that you understand the behavior, it is time to discuss practical solutions to the issue.

Controlling the Level Being Sent to the Channel

There are a number of things that could possibly cause a channel's level to go into the red on the meter. Although this rarely happens with Logic Pro's software instruments, it is not uncommon for third-party developers to design some of their presets to be very hot. When we hear things louder, we tend to think they sound better, so perhaps that is why they do that.

The solution to this issue is pretty simple. Go into the GUI and turn down the output, and then save the patch so you do not have to deal with this in the future.

Many times the problem is created by a plug-in, such as an EQ, amp simulator, or compressor. When you use an EQ to raise certain frequencies, the output will get louder. All software EQs will have a fader or knob called Master Gain, Gain, Output, and so on that allows you to compensate for this issue.

In Figure 19.3, in a UAD-1 Neve 1073, it is the red knob.

Figure 19.3 The UAD-1's Neve 1073 GUI.

The same is true of compressors. If you add compression, you may well lower or raise the output of the sound, so there is a fader or knob that is commonly referred to as a "makeup" gain stage. In Logic's Compressor, which you see in Figure 19.4, it is simply called Gain.

Figure 19.4 The Logic Compressor's GUI.

Am I saying that if, with Pre Fader Metering turned on, you see some channels occasionally going into the red, you are getting distortion and creating a massive problem? No. I have no problem with, for example, sharp snare hits going into the red. What I am saying is that if all or most of your channels are consistently going into the red, you are not paying enough attention to your gain structure, and particularly if you are using a lot of third-party FX plug-ins and software instruments, your mix will not be all that it can be. Even in a 32-bit float app such as Logic, IMHO, more conservative gain practices lead to a more open and better-sounding mix. Also, you are forming bad habits that potentially will get you into trouble when you work in a fixed-point app, such as Pro Tools or a hybrid analog/ITB system.

An ounce of prevention is worth a pound of cure.

Tutorial 20: Old-School Punch-In Audio Recording with Logic Pro 9

Logic Pro 9 has continued to make advances in its ease of use for audio recording and editing with many innovative features, such as the take folder concept with Swipe Comping. However, there are many users out there who simply want to work in a similar manner to the way they have always worked with consoles and tape recorders. In this tutorial we will explore ways to come as close to that as possible.

At the time I am writing this, there are changes in LP9 that we are simply stuck with. The take folder feature when cycle recording cannot be turned off. The behavior for the key commands for Record, Record Toggle, and Record/Record Toggle has also changed a little.

Setting Up Logic Pro 9 for Punching In and Out on a Track without Stopping, Tape-Recorder Style

Usually, my preferred way of recording vocalists is to do several complete takes and then edit a comp. It gives the performer a chance to create whole performances emotionally. With great singers this works well. However, there is a limited window of opportunity between the time the singer's voice is warmed up, open, and resonant and the time it starts to get tired and lose some overtone richness. Also, we can't always work with great singers.

So, frequently, I want to do things the way I did with a tape recorder, which is to record a take and then punch in and out on the parts I want to replace, sometimes without stopping the sequencer. Here is a scenario.

Susie comes to my studio to record her vocal on a gorgeous arrangement I have done for her of the classic Leon Russell song, "A Song for You." After she warms up, I start to record several takes of hers on separate audio tracks, stopping the sequencer in between, as I do not wish to use the take folder methodology. After a few takes, it becomes apparent to me that one of the takes is mostly really good and that from here on in I am not likely to get performances that sound as good.

In my tape-recorder days, I would say to her, "Susie, I love what you did on Take 3. Please sing along from the beginning, and I will punch you in and out where I wish."

In order to work well this way, there are several things I recommend you do:

1. Open the Key Commands window (Option+K) and in the Search field, type Record. You should see a window similar to Figure 20.1, unless you have already changed the key command assignments.

2. Click on the Learn by Key Label button and go to the Record line and hit Delete, which will remove the default key command of asterisk.

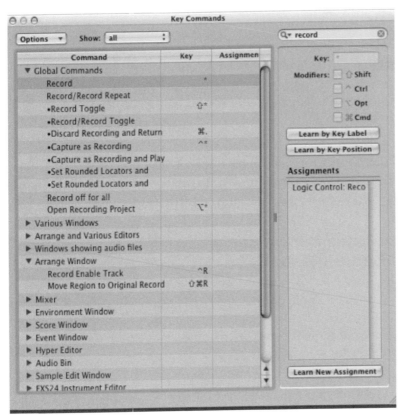

Figure 20.1 The Key Commands window before you change key command assignments.

3.   Go to the line for Record/Record Toggle and assign the asterisk key to it. Remember to then click on the Learn by Key Label button. The window should now appear like Figure 20.2.

Key commands are global, so this will be in all your projects. Personally, I see no downside to this even when you are not recording in this manner.

---

4.   While holding down the Control key, click and hold the mouse button on the Record button in the Transport bar and check Punch on the Fly. Do not be concerned that Record is checked rather than Record//Record Toggle, because we have already taken care of that. See Figure 20.3.

This is a project setting, not a preference, so it is not global, and therefore you may want to set it this way in your templates.

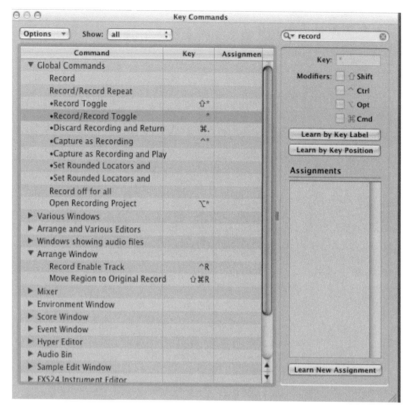

Figure 20.2   The Key Commands window after you change key command assignments.

5.   The final step to set up Logic to emulate the old tape recorder style of recording is to set Logic's recording to Replace mode. In the Transport bar, click on the X and it will turn orange, indicating that Logic is in Replace mode. This means that when you punch in, Logic will replace the old audio with the new audio.

VERY IMPORTANT! You are now recording destructively, so it is a good idea to make a copy of the audio file before you start punching in and out.

Tape Recorder–Style Recording

So we start playback of the project, and after Jay's beautiful intro (shameless, I know), we hear Susie's vocal come in for the first verse. "I've been so many places, in my life and time. I've sung a lot of songs, and I've made some bad rhymes." (Very nice!)

"I've acted out my life in stages, with 10,000 people watching..." (Er, not so good.) "But we're alone now, and I'm singing this song for you." (Also good.)

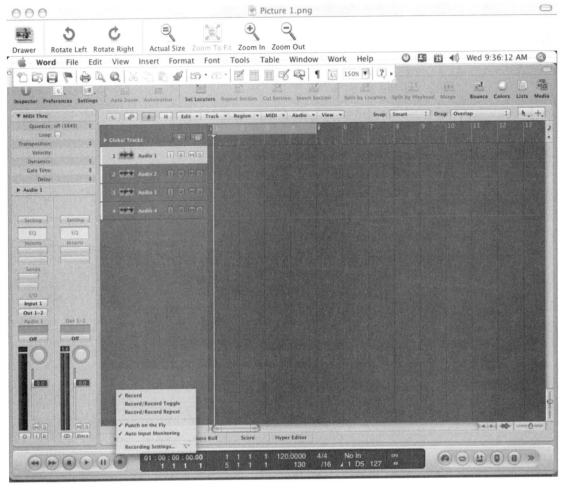

Figure 20.3   Enabling Punch on the Fly in the Transport bar.

At this point, we can continue to make notes for the places where we want to punch in and out for the whole song or just deal with this verse. We will deal with just this verse.

1.   Press the Return key to begin playback while Susie sings along.

2.   In the space between the second and third lines, hit the asterisk button, and Logic will begin replacing the old audio with the new. Not so good? Hit Command+Z to undo it. Now that is something I could *not* do on a tape recorder. Thank you, Apple!

3.   Try again. Hooray Susie, you nailed it!

4.   Continue to do this where necessary for the rest of the song.

See Figure 20.4 to see the audio track with punches in and out. They are blank because I did not actually hook up a microphone—it was not necessary to demonstrate the methods.

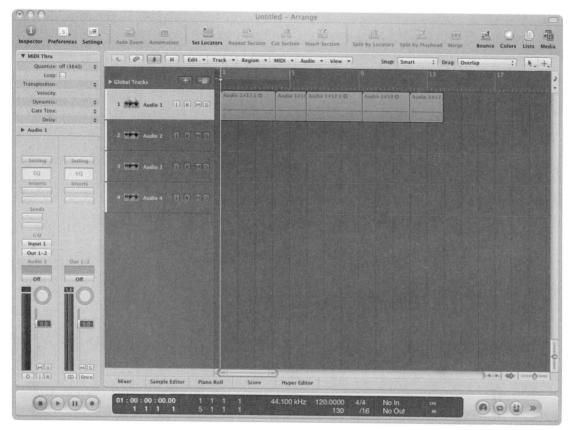

Figure 20.4   An audio track with multiple punches in and out.

We now have a cohesive vocal take that we are happy with. Of course, nothing stops us from cutting and pasting together sections from this take and other takes where we feel we need to. It is also possible—depending on how tight the space is that you want to punch in/out on and your skills—that there will be some pops and clicks to which you will want to apply crossfading to resolve.

For me, there is only one fly in the ointment with this method in Logic Pro 9, and that relates to the metronome click. When you punch in, you will lose the sound of the first click. This is not a problem if the singer does not need to hear a click; simply turn off the metronome. Hopefully, Apple will resolve this in a future update.

Newer-School Punch-In Recording

Those who did not come up in the business back in the tape days may be flying by the seat of their pants a little more than they are comfortable with. So they might want to hedge their bets a little and punch in specific areas. In Logic Pro 9, this is called *Autopunch*, and it is quite simple.

Back to Susie. In the bridge she nicely sings the first line. Sadly, she blows the next line. We determine that the second line falls in the timeline at position 43 4 4 176 and needs to be out at 45 3 4 128.

1.   In the Transport bar, click the Autopunch icon, just to the left of the Replace mode button. It turns red, and you see an area in the Bar ruler set to Autopunch, but not where we want it. The area is determined by the left and right punch locators, which we need to change.

2.   While holding down the Control key, press the mouse button on the Transport bar and choose Customize Transport Bar. This opens the dialog box; under Display, check Sample Rate or Punch Locators, as you see in Figure 20.5. Click OK, and they will now appear in the Transport between the left and right locators and the project tempo.

Figure 20.5 The dialog box for enabling viewing of the punch locators in the Transport bar.

3.   Type in the proper position for the punch-in spot in the left punch locator, and then do the same for the right punch locator for the punch-out spot. See Figure 20.6.

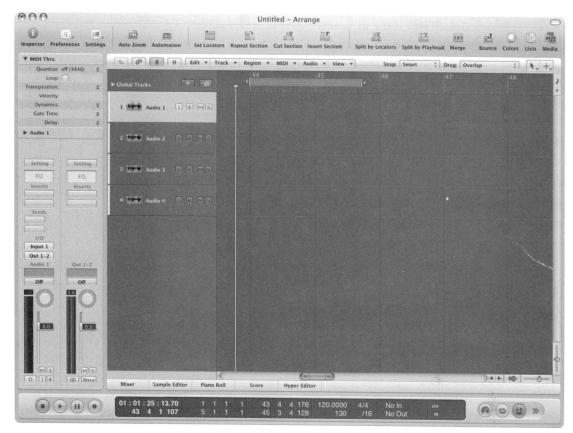

Figure 20.6   The Transport bar with visible punch locators.

You can now start recording wherever you like in the project, and Logic will leave the audio material intact until it punches in and out at the desired spots. If you wish, you can also set a cycle area for a little before and after the desired area, but then if you record without stopping, you enter the wonderful world of take folders, which is what we are trying to avoid in this tutorial.

Tutorial 21: Creating a Customized Click Track

Logic Pro 9 has added a ton of long-requested improvements, but sadly, one thing that remains little changed is its click track implementation. Whether you are using the built-in KlopfGeist as the sound source for your metronome or a hardware module, if your Logic project is in 4/4, the metronome will be playing quarter notes. If it is in 12/8, it will be playing eighth notes. And let me tell you, if the project is in 12/8 at a fast tempo, hearing all those eighth notes is distracting as hell. Clearly, dotted quarter notes would be a better choice, but Logic does not give you that option.

Also, you may wish to record the click to export along with stems to bring in a Pro Tools session for recording additional live musicians and/or mixing and making sure that everything is as it should be.

The answer is to create your own click track.

Setting Up Logic Pro 9 for Creating a Customized Click Track and Exporting It as Audio

Since the KlopfGeist is a software instrument, you can use it as a sound source for your click track, but I prefer to use a cross stick snare in a drum kit loaded in the EXS24. Usually you would do this in an existing project, but for demonstration purposes we will create a new project with some meter changes and even tempo changes.

1. Open a new empty project and create one software instrument with Open Library checked.

2. In the Library tab, navigate to 04 Drums & Percussion > 01 Acoustic Drum Kits > Studio Tight Kit and click on it. It will load into the software instrument track. See Figure 21.1.

3. Close the Media area.

4. Play C#1, and you will hear the cross stick snare sound.

5. Go to File > Project Settings > Metronome (or access it from the Settings button in the Toolbar), and the window you see in Figure 21.2 will appear. If they are checked, uncheck both Click While Recording and Click While Playing.

6. Now if you start playback or go into record, you will not hear a click.

Let's set up a sample "composition" by creating some meter changes. This can be done, and Apple teaches students in their Pro Training books to do this in global tracks. For the sake of this tutorial, I will assume that you know how to do this, but I prefer to do this in the same manner I did before global tracks were introduced.

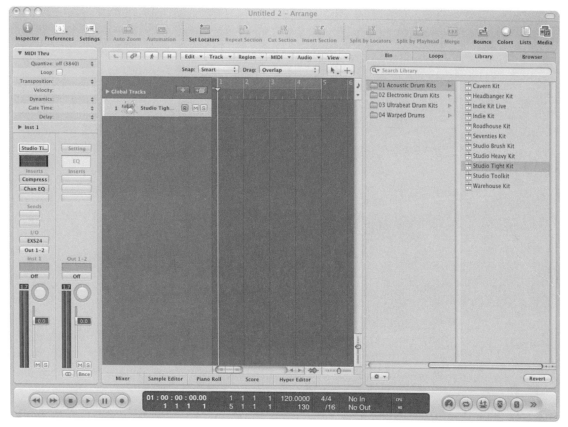

Figure 21.1   Choosing an EXS24 drum kit from the Library.

1.   Make sure that you are right at the beginning of the project. In the Transport bar, the meter defaults to 4/4. Hold down the numerator and drag it up to 12, and then drag the denominator to 8, so that it now looks like Figure 21.3.

2.   Use your Go To Position key command (the MVP of key commands, IMHO) to advance in the timeline to Bar 7 (or do so however else you prefer).

3.   Change the meter to 9/8.

4.   Go to Bar 13 and change the meter to 4/4.

5.   Set the length of the project to 16 full bars by double-clicking on the number under the tempo display in the Transport bar and typing in 17. See Figure 21.4.

Creating a MIDI Region for the Click and Exporting It as Audio

This process sounds more complicated than it actually is.

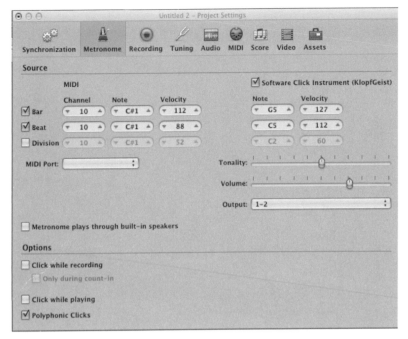

Figure 21.2   The Metronome Settings window.

01 : 00 : 00 : 00.00			1	1	1	1	120.0000	12/8	No In	CPU
1	1	1	1	5	1	1	1	130	/16	No Out	HD

Figure 21.3   12/8 meter in the Transport bar.

13	1	1	1	44.100 kHz	120.0000	4/4	No In	CPU
13	2	1	1		17	/16	No Out	HD

Figure 21.4   The project length set to 16 full bars (17).

1. Create a blank region with the Pencil tool and drag its length to the length of the song. You could also do this with the Event Float.

2. In the MIDI editor of your choice, you will enter the MIDI notes to create the click. I prefer the Score Editor.

3. Open the Score Editor with the Score tab and, from the Part Box, drag in a dotted quarter note to C#1.

4. Highlight the note so that it is blinking and, either by key command or under the Score Editor's Functions menu, choose Copy MIDI Events. You need to Copy Merge from left locator 1 1 1 1 to right locator 1 4 1 1 to position 1 4 1 1 forty-two times to bring you to the end of the dotted quarter note clicks, as you see in Figure 21.5.

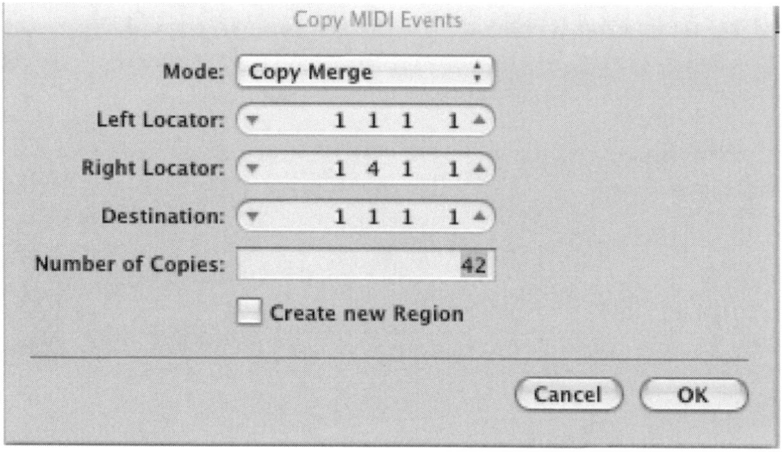

Figure 21.5   Copying MIDI events for the 12/6 and 9/8 sections.

5.   Now from the Part Box, drag in a quarter note to C#1 at the downbeat of Bar 13.

6.   Use Copy MIDI Events to Copy Merge the blinking quarter note 15 times from left locator 13 1 1 1 to right locator 13 2 1 1 to position 13 2 1 1, as you see in Figure 21.6

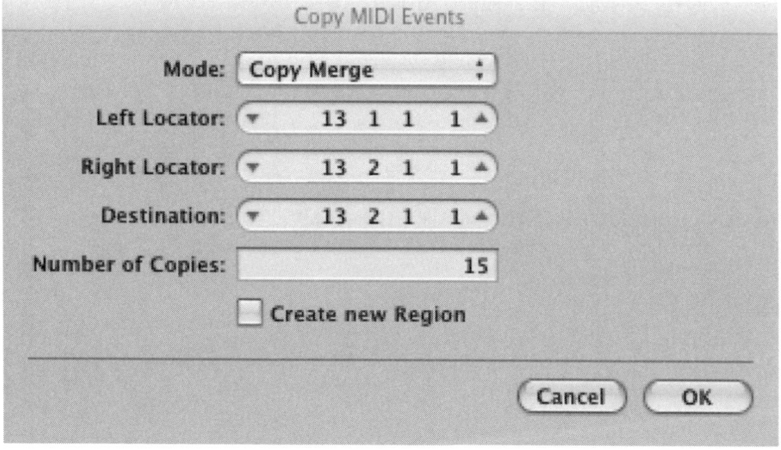

Figure 21.6   Copying MIDI events for the 4/4 section.

7.   Close the Score Editor and play the project. You now have a customized MIDI click that will respond to any tempo changes you enter into the project, as this is MIDI.

Only one optional step remains, which is to turn it into an audio file for exporting, which you can do by simply exporting the track, along with your other stems or separately, by highlighting the track(s) and navigating to File > Export > Track as Audio File or by Bounce Track In Place, if you prefer.

Tutorial 22: Using Parallel Compression in Logic Pro 9

This technique is also sometimes referred to as the New York or New York City compression trick, and it is a great way to fatten up sounds. Most commonly, it is used on drums.

This technique involves mixing compressed and uncompressed versions of the same sounds to give you the punch of the compressed version while maintaining the dynamics of the uncompressed original sound.

Setting Up for Parallel Compression

Ideally, you would do this with discrete drum parts, but we will use an Apple Loop for this tutorial.

1.   Open a new project with one audio track.

2.   In the Media area, search for the blue Apple Loop named Funked Out Drumset 01. Loop it, play it back, and listen. See Figure 22.1.

3.   On the Audio 1 track's channel strip, assign the first send to Bus 1, and an aux will be created with Bus 1 as its input.

4.   On the Audio 1 track's channel strip, assign the second send to Bus 2, and an aux will be created with Bus 2 as its input. The Mixer should now appear as in Figure 22.2.

5.   Insert a Compressor on Aux 2 and load the preset named Type R Tight Drum Kit. See Figure 22.3.

6.   Adjust the Compressor's attack, threshold, gain, and other parameters to different settings and choose the ones that you find aesthetically pleasing.

7.   On the Audio 1 track's channel strip, hold down the mouse in the output rectangle and assign the output to No Output.

8.   Play it back and listen, and notice that there is no sound, as nothing is reaching the output.

9.   While continuing playback, drag the Bus 1 send knob gradually to the right, and you increasingly will hear the uncompressed signal of the loop going to the output through the aux that has no plug-in. Drag it all the way back to the left, and the sound will disappear again.

10.   While continuing playback, drag the Bus 2 send knob gradually to the right, and you increasingly will hear the compressed signal of the loop going to the output through the aux that has the Compressor. Drag it all the way back to the left, and the sound will disappear again.

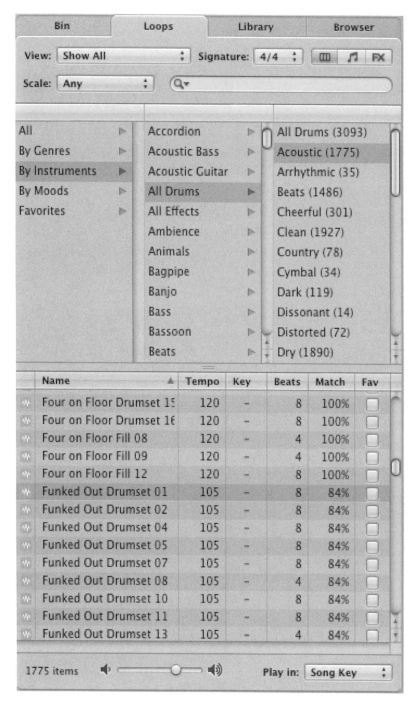

Figure 22.1   The Funked Out Drumset 01 loop in the Loop Browser.

Figure 22.2   The Mixer with Audio 1 and the two auxes.

11.   By adjusting the two send knobs, you now have the ability to mix the compressed signal with the uncompressed signal, and of course, this can be fully automated.

If you use a latency-inducing compressor, such as UAD-1's Fairchild or Logic Pro's own Multipressor, you may hear some latency between the compressed and uncompressed signals. Setting LP9's Plug-In Delay Compensation to All should fix it. If it still is not acceptable to you, try adding another instance of the same compressor on the other aux and simply bypassing it.

An Even Easier Method

Although I personally prefer the first method because it allows the user a somewhat greater amount of control, some of you may opt for this method because it is so fast and easy. (This is only possible, however, if the compressor of your choice has an adjustable wet/dry mix.)

Figure 22.3   Loading the Type R Tight Drum Kit preset in Logic's Compressor.

1. Open a new project with one audio track.

2. In the Media area, search for the blue Apple Loop named Funked Out Drumset 01. Loop it, play it back, and listen. Refer to Figure 22.1.

3. On the Audio 1 track's channel strip, assign the first send to Bus 1, and an aux will be created with Bus 1 as its input.

4. Insert a Compressor on Aux 1 and load the same preset we loaded previously. Refer to Figure 22.3.

5. Adjust the Compressor's attack, threshold, gain, and so on to different settings and choose the ones that you find aesthetically pleasing.

6. In the lower-left of the Compressor's GUI, click the disclosure triangle, and you should now see the screen shown in Figure 22.4.

Figure 22.4   The Output Mix section of the Compressor.

7.   In the Mix rectangle of the Output Mix section, you can now simply choose the percentage of dry to compressed signal you desire, and in tandem with the fader on the Audio 1 track, control it. This can, of course, also be automated.

Could it be easier?

Tutorial 23: Using Logic Pro 9's Track-Based Automation and Region-Based Automation

The preference for one or the other workflow is yet another of the most debated topics of discussion among Logic Pro users, particularly those who like to work with multi-timbral instances. Back in the olden days, when Logic Pro was an Emagic product, there was only Hyper Draw, a MIDI-controlled region-based automation. While it worked, it was not as powerful as we would have liked, and it was agreed that Logic Pro needed its own host automation. Then a debate ensued among the beta testers (I was one) as to whether it would be better to have a more robust region-based automation system or a track-based one, like Pro Tools has. In the end, Emagic decided to go with track-based automation.

As mentioned in the tutorial on multi-timbral versus stereo instances, this creates a problem for volume automation of MIDI channels. (This issue is less relevant for EXS24 libraries, as the EXS24 is not multi-timbral.) Also, many Kontakt and Play libraries make use of cc1 (mod wheel) and cc11 (expression) to do volume changes that are more subtle and also affect other elements, such as timbre and vibrato. So many of us who use these libraries have adopted a hybrid real-time workflow of using Hyper Draw for MIDI channel volume automation while using the track-based automation as we would a trim on a console, and it is pretty powerful.

Using CC1 or CC11 to Automate Volume on MIDI Channels

Let's explore the CPU and RAM usage impact of each method.

1.   Open a new project with one multi-timbral software instrument track with three MIDI channels.

2.   Instantiate an instance of any software instrument that has multi-timbral capability and patches that respond to cc1. I will be using Kontakt 4 and loading three cello articulations from Audiobro's LA Scoring Strings library. They all default to cc11 volume automation very expressively. See Figure 23.1.

3.   I will now record a cello part in real time, playing my keyboard while automating cc1 from my expression pedal. I will switch tracks using the down arrow on my computer keyboard.

4.   Okay, the result is what you see in Figure 23.2. Notice that you can see that there is volume automation by the green nodes in the regions. And unlike track-based automation cc7, if they were to play simultaneously, Kontakt 4 would not start sputtering and going crazy.

5.   Let's get a better look. Press Command+A to select all the regions. Under the View menu, navigate to Hyper Draw > Modulation. Now you can see all the region automation and edit it here or in the Piano Roll, Hyper Editor, or Event List. See Figure 23.3.

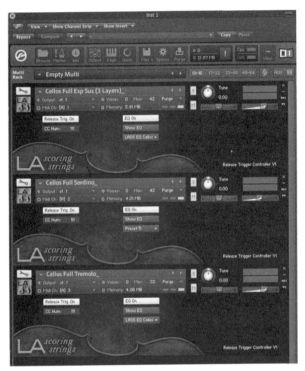

Figure 23.1   LASS cello patches in a Kontakt 4 multi.

Figure 23.2   Regions on several MIDI channel tracks with cc1 volume automation in the Arrange window.

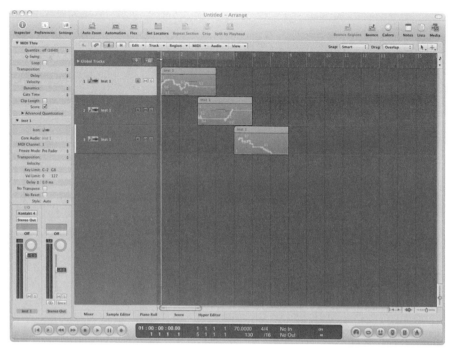

Figure 23.3   The regions with Hyper Draw view.

So now I open Logic Pro 9's track-based automation by pressing A. I click in a node and set my level. I can add more nodes to refine the overall level of the AU itself without disturbing the Hyper Draw automation I have already performed. I can even do this in Latch or Touch mode in real time if that is my preference. I personally like to do this on a separate Arrange track, so I use the key command for creating a track New with Same Channel Strip/Instrument and assign the MIDI channel to All so that I can see the track-based automation and Hyper Draw automation simultaneously, as you see in Figure 23.4.

As I said, this workflow is either necessary or not depending on whether you prefer to use stereo or multi-timbral instances and whether the given library has additional features where cc1 and cc11 bring heightened musicality to the table. In today's libraries and software instruments, frequently they do.

I love this workflow and recommend you take it out for a test drive.

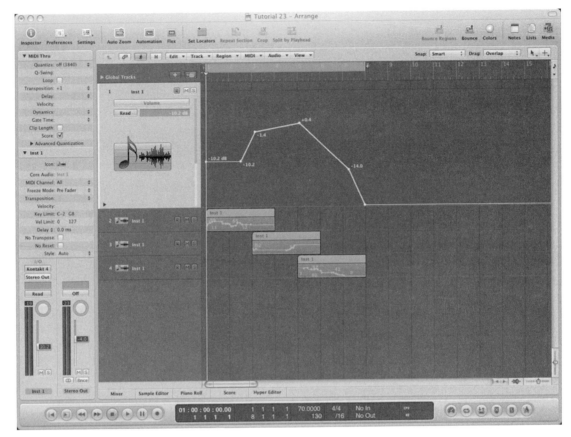

Figure 23.4   Track-based and region-based automation.

Tutorial 24: Using UAD Cards with Logic Pro 9

In the opinion of many, myself included, for their UAD-1 and UAD-2 cards, Universal Audio has created some of the finest native plug-ins available. They can hold their own with comparable respected TDM plug-ins. Their emulations of classic compressors, vintage EQs, and their Precision series of mastering plug-ins continue to attract many users. Although the additional DSP power provided by the card that is required to run the plug-ins is no longer as powerful an incentive, in this day of more and more powerful Macs, there are many of us who would say that you would have to pry them out of our cold, dead hands.

They do present some challenges for Logic users, however, as many of the plug-ins introduce a fair amount of latency when instantiated on auxes, busses, and outputs. This issue is not limited to UAD plug-ins. Logic's own Adaptive Limiter and Multipressor also add some latency, as do some other third-party plug-ins.

The good news is that Logic Pro 8/9's plug-in delay compensation, hereafter referred to as PDC, is much improved from that of Logic Pro 7.

Latency is not a problem for those of us who think in terms of a compose, arrange, then mix workflow, because by and large we wait until we are through playing in parts before mixing with latency-inducing plug-ins, but it *is* an issue for "I mix as I compose" guys.

1. Open the UAD Meter and Control Panel. Click on the Configuration tab and make sure that you check Force Logic to Use "Live Mode" for Tracks with UAD-1 Plugins (see Figure 24.1). Although this is less necessary with UAD-2 cards than UAD-1 cards, and indeed may even change in the future, at the time I am writing this, it is still advisable for both.

2. Open a new LP9 empty project with three stereo software instrument tracks.

3. In the Toolbar, click on the Preferences button and choose the Audio Preferences. Click on the General tab and notice that halfway down is an area dealing with Plug-In Latency.

4. Click and hold the mouse down in the Compensation rectangle and see that there are three possible settings: Off, Audio and Software Instrument Tracks, and All. For now, set it to Off and leave the Low Latency Mode button unchecked. See Figure 24.2.

5. Close the Preferences.

6. In the first software instrument track, load Ultrabeat, which will load a default kit and open the GUI. Close the GUI. Start Logic's sequencer in play and then play against the click from your MIDI controller, and there will be no latency.

7. If you own it or you can run it in demo mode, load a UAD stereo Fairchild in the first insert slot. Start Logic's sequencer in play and again play against the click from your MIDI controller, and there will be a small amount of latency.

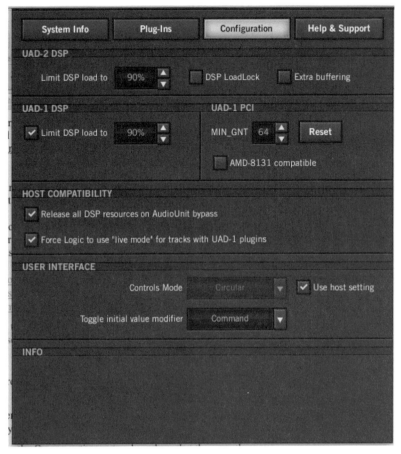

Figure 24.1 The Configuration tab in the UAD Meter and Control Panel.

8. Load a second UAD plug-in, such as a Pultec, in the second insert slot. Start Logic's sequencer in play and again play against the click from your MIDI controller, and there will be a greater amount of latency. See Figure 24.3.

9. Return to your Audio Preferences and change the PDC setting to Audio and Software Instrument Tracks. Start Logic's sequencer in play and again play against the click from your MIDI controller, and there will be considerably less latency. Very tolerable.

Using UAD Plug-Ins on Auxes and Outputs

This is where latency starts to require a little more thought.

1. In the Mixer, click on the plus sign to create an aux with Bus 1 as an input.

2. In the first insert slot of the aux, load in a UAD-1 plug-in. I am using the LA-3A compressor.

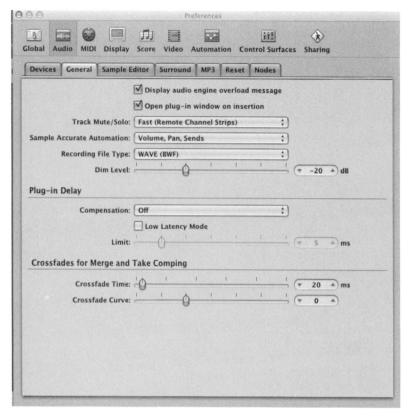

Figure 24.2   The General tab of the Audio Preferences.

3.   In the first insert slot of Output 1–2, load in one or two more plug-ins. I am using a Precision EQ and a Precision Limiter. See Figure 24.4. Close the Mixer.

4.   Start Logic's sequencer and again play against the click from your MIDI controller, and there will be an intolerable amount of latency.

5.   Return to your Audio Preferences, change the PDC setting to All, and check the Low Latency Mode option. Start Logic's sequencer in play and again play against the click from your MIDI controller. There will be no latency, but you will not hear the effect of the plug-ins. With these settings, Logic temporarily creates an alternate output path that avoids the latency-inducing plug-ins while you are playing in the parts. Simply bypassing the plug-ins will not achieve this.

6.   If the Low Latency Mode button is in the Transport bar, it will be orange colored when on. Toggle it off. See Figure 24.5.

7.   Go into the Ultrabeat GUI and in the lower-right, drag the pattern 1 (C-1) sq to the Arrange area at Bar 1 and loop it. See Figure 24.6.

Figure 24.3   The Ultrabeat channel strip in the Inspector with two UAD plug-ins on inserts.

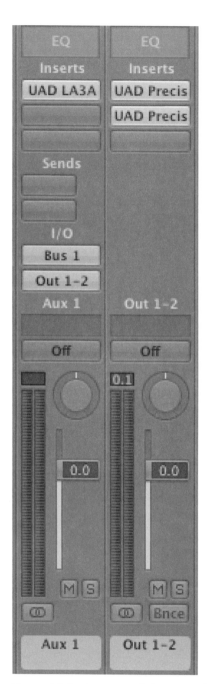

Figure 24.4   An aux and Output 1–2 in the Mixer with UAD plug-ins loaded in inserts.

Figure 24.5   Low Latency Mode toggled on in the Transport bar.

Figure 24.6   The Pattern area of the Ultrabeat GUI.

8.   Start playback in Logic and pull down the UB fader so that you can hear it against the click. It will be perfectly in sync.

9.   Select the Inst 2 track and open the Media area. Choose the Loops tab.

10.   Click on the Bass tab and in the list, scroll down to the green Apple Loop named Bread and Butter Bass 29.

11.   Drag it to the Inst 2 track at Bar 1 and loop it.

12.   Click Reset in the Loop Browser, click on Electronic, and scroll down to the green Apple Loop named Euro Move Synth 01.

13.   Drag it to the Inst 3 track at Bar 1 and loop it.

14.   Start playback in Logic, and they all will be perfectly in sync.

And man, those plug-ins sound good!

Logic Pro 9 and the Outside World: Techniques for Integrating Third-Party Software and Hardware with Logic Pro 9

Man (or woman) cannot live by Logic Pro 9 alone. Okay, maybe he (or she) can, but it is a lot more fun if you integrate some of the wonderful and affordable software and hardware available into your workflow. Once again, preparation is key, and the tutorials in this chapter were written with that in mind.

Tutorial 25: Using Kontakt 3.5 (or 4) as a Standalone with Logic Pro 9

Logic Pro 9 EXS24 software sampler is terrifically CPU-efficient and well integrated into Logic. Additionally, it has an impressive number of great sample libraries available for it, either in native format or through conversion.

Sometimes available libraries written for Native Instruments' Kontakt will take advantage of its powerful scripting capabilities. This will sometimes make Kontakt your choice of sampler. This tutorial assumes that you have a basic understanding of how to use Kontakt, at least as a plug-in in Logic. I will be using Kontakt 3.5 with its new Memory Server feature, which allows it to address RAM outside of Logic Pro 9, in a similar fashion to the EXS24. Kontakt 4 has been released, with many new features and enhancements, but as 3.5 is still at this point more commonly in use and the techniques described here should not be affected, I will use 3.5 for this tutorial.

Running Kontakt outside of Logic allows you to utilize your RAM more fully, as each loaded Kontakt instance uses some of Logic's virtual memory. Of course, sometime in the not-too-distant future, a 64-bit Kontakt 4 inside the now 64-bit Logic Pro 9 will render this factor moot. However, there is still benefit to running Kontakt outside of Logic, as it gives you the advantage of not having to wait for the instruments to reload when changing Logic projects, which is especially handy for film projects.

Downloading and Installing Soundflower

Cycling '74's Soundflower, a virtual audio interface that will appear in Core Audio as if it were a hardware audio interface, is a free application that allows Kontakt to be loaded outside of Logic and to "speak" to Logic. Let's download and install it.

1. Go to the Cycling '74 website at www.cycling74.com and click the Downloads link under the Support category.

2. Download and install Soundflower and Soundflowerbed.

3. Restart your computer.

In my previous book, at this point I described that now that Soundflower was installed, it was necessary to create an Aggregate Device with Soundflower and your audio interface. Happily, this is no longer so with Logic Pro 9 and Snow Leopard.

Setting Up Kontakt 3.5 as a Standalone

We will use Kontakt 3.5 and its included library to demonstrate this technique.

1. Open Kontakt 3.5.

2. Under the Kontakt 3.5 menu, choose Preferences.

3. Select the Audio tab. Where you see Device, hold the mouse down and choose Sound-flower (16 ch) (16 In, 18 Out). See Figure 25.1.

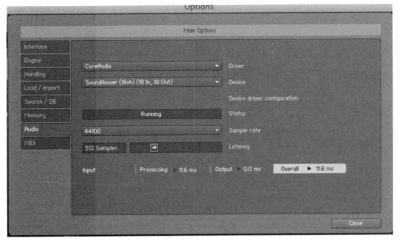

Figure 25.1   Kontakt 3.5 with a properly set up Audio tab.

4. Click the MIDI tab, and in the Output Interface section, make sure that the IAC Driver, Bus 1, is set to Port A in the Inputs Interface and that everything is off in the Outputs. Click Close to exit.

5. Load some sounds or a bank into Kontakt. For this example I will load four instruments from the VSL included instruments: Violins, Violas, Celli, and Double Bass.

6. The four instruments are automatically mapped to MIDI channels 1–4. Assign the outputs to St. 1–4. (You might have to create 2–4 if they are not already.) Configure the outputs to Built-In-SF 2 and 3, 4 and 5, and so on. See Figure 25.2 for an example of a properly set up main window in Kontakt 3.5.

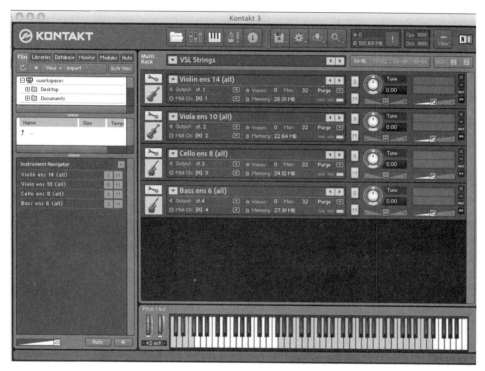

Figure 25.2   The newly created Kontakt 3 multi with MIDI channel and output assignments.

Setting Up Logic Pro 9

We will now set up Logic Pro 9 properly to use with Kontakt 3.5 as a standalone. You might already have a template, but for this tutorial I will assume that you do not, so the same principles will apply.

There are two good routing approaches here. One method is to use the MIDI instruments to play in the parts and monitor the audio through audio tracks with the proper input assignments and input monitoring enabled or create input channel strips in the Environment. That is a perfectly valid approach, but I prefer to utilize Logic Pro 9's little-understood and under-utilized External instrument plug-in, which is a software instrument that allows you to assign a corresponding MIDI instrument and audio input right in one GUI.

1. Open a new project in Logic Pro from the Empty Project template and create four software instruments.

2. Click the Preferences button in the Toolbar and select Audio Preferences.

3. In the Devices tab, where you choose an audio interface, choose the Built-In Output and Soundflower Input and click Apply Changes. See Figure 25.3.

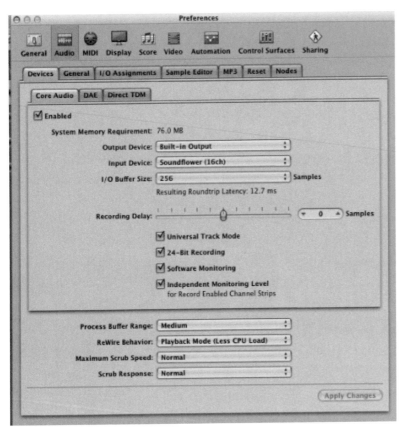

Figure 25.3   Logic Pro 9's Audio preferences.

4. The next step is *very important* in order to prevent an unintended MIDI loop. Press Command+8 to open the Environment and navigate to the Clicks & Ports layer. Create an instrument (MIDI) and assign its port to Off. Name it Dead End or something similar. Draw a cable from the IAC Bus 1 on the physical output to the new instrument (see Figure 25.4).

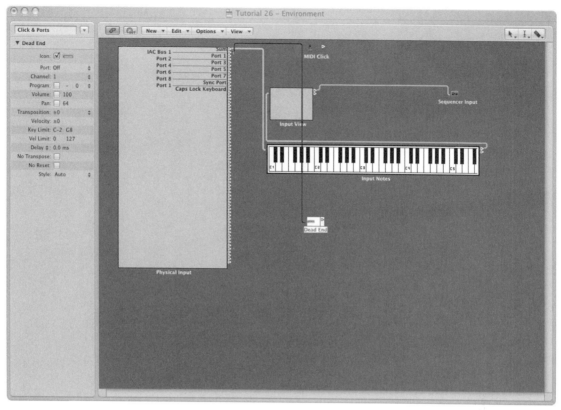

Figure 25.4   The Clicks & Ports Environment layer.

5.   Press Command+8 to open the Environment and navigate to the MIDI Instruments layer. Create a new multi instrument, enable the first four subchannels, and name it VSL Strings. Make sure that its port assignment is IAC Bus 1. See Figure 25.5.

6.   Open an External software instrument on Inst 1 and assign its MIDI Destination to the multi instrument's Channel 1 and its Input to 1-2, which correspond to the first Sound-flower inputs. See Figure 25.6.

7.   Open an External software instrument on Inst 2 and assign its MIDI Destination to the multi instrument's Channel 2 and its Input to 3-4, which correspond to the next Sound-flower inputs.

8.   Open an External software instrument on Inst 3 and assign its MIDI Destination to the multi instrument's Channel 3 and its Input to 5-6, which correspond to the next Sound-flower inputs.

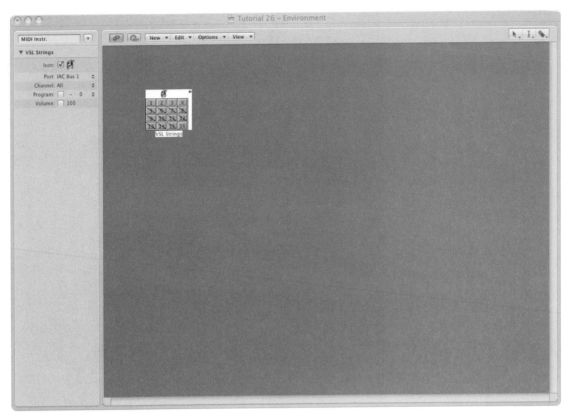

Figure 25.5   The MIDI Instruments Environment layer.

Figure 25.6   The External instrument with MIDI channel and inputs assigned.

9.   Open an External software instrument on Inst 4 and assign its MIDI Destination to the multi instrument's Channel 4 and its Input to 7-8, which correspond to the next Sound-flower inputs.

Save this as part of one of your templates or a new template, and you are good to go!

Tutorial 26: Using Key Switches to Change Instruments in a Kontakt 4 Program Bank in Logic Pro 9

Many libraries have patches with the ability to change articulations in Kontakt through use of key switching, and users of Vienna Instruments and other libraries like this workflow. The advantages are obvious. You require fewer tracks in your project, and you can switch from, for example, a legato violin to a pizzicato violin in real time. There are, however, also some disadvantages.

Let us say I play C0, which in this library triggers legato, and I continue to play for four bars and without stopping hit B0, which triggers pizzicato, and continue playing. If I play back from the beginning (and I have the project setting for MIDI notes set to chase—which, by the way, should be the default or a pref rather than a project setting), all is fine. Now, however, when I get to Bar 7, I hit Stop and want to edit playing back from Bar 3. I hear pizz instead of legato. Grrrr.

Okay, so there is a simple workaround. In the Score Editor I choose all those low key-switch notes and Note Force Legato (selected to selected). So now when I go back to Bar 3 and play, it chases and plays legato *but* only from the second note—the first note still plays pizz. Grrrr.

The other disadvantage is that some great libraries are simply not set up this way, as they are using key switching for other tasks. A good example is Audiobro's wonderful new LA Scoring Strings. Many of its users, including its creator, Andrew Keresztes, like to have a separate track for each articulation and are undaunted by a massive track count. The answer is to load articulations into an instrument bank in Kontakt 4 (or 3.5) and set up Logic to convert keys on the controller to send program changes. Program changes chase beautifully anywhere in a project. Unfortunately, these "faux" program changes triggered by key switches behave more like key switches than program changes, so the same disadvantages apply, which is why triggering program changes from a controller is a better workflow, IMHO.

But for those of you who nonetheless prefer key switches and are not annoyed by the attendant issues, here we go. This is more than a little geeky to set up. While I probably should take full credit for this and let you think I am an Environment genius, the sad truth is that I required the help of my good friend Peter Schwartz, perhaps the ultimate Environment and MIDI freak, for most of what you will now learn here. Thank you, Peter, for allowing me to use this.

Creating Key Switches to Trigger Program Changes in Kontakt 4

Open a new empty project and create one software instrument. Instantiate Kontakt 4 (or 3.5).

1. In the Files menu, choose New Instrument Bank. See Figure 26.1.

2. Either from the Browser or by dragging in from the Quick-Load menu in Kontakt 4, I will now load in four easily discernible articulations from LASS Violin C group, starting with slot 001. (If you are using the Quick-Load menu, do not click them, or they will be loaded

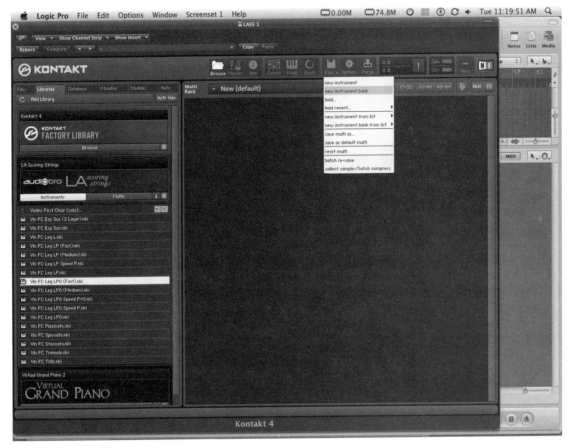

Figure 26.1   Creating a new instrument bank in Kontakt 4.

outside the instrument bank.) I am using Vlns C leg LP (medium), Vlns C Pizzicato, Vlns C Tremolo, and Vlns C Trills.

3.   It is important to set the MIDI channel to Omni. The Kontakt 4 instance should now appear as you see in Figure 26.2.

4.   Close the Browser but leave the instrument bank open.

5.   In the instrument bank, choose an articulation and play your keyboard with one hand. Continue to play and click on the different articulations, and the sound will change instantly. Now we can change articulations simply by inserting program change messages in the Event List Editor, but we want to do this key-switching style.

Cool, here comes the geeky stuff!

1.   Close the K4 instance or simply move it out of the way. Navigate to the Clicks & Ports layer of the Environment.

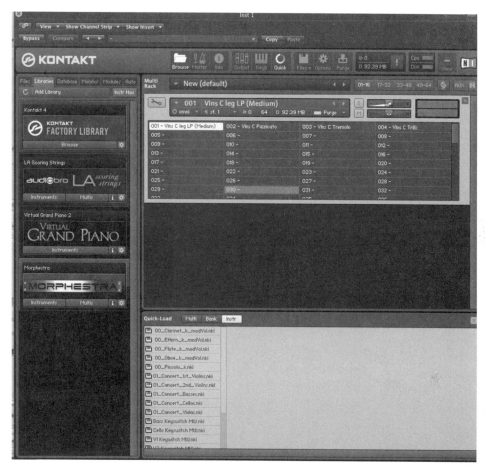

Figure 26.2   LASS Violin C articulations in a Kontakt 4 instrument bank.

2. Under the New menu, choose Transformer and double-click on it to open it. It defaults to a Transformer mode named Apply Operation and Let Non-Matching Events Pass Thru, which fortunately happens to be the one we want to utilize. See Figure 26.3.

3. In the Transformer's Conditions section, change the Status from ALL to =, and a box will appear underneath it to select the kind of event that = refers to. It defaults to Note, which is what we want.

4. Leave Channel set to All. Change Pitch from All to Inside and set its range from C0 to B0, as these notes are the bottom octave of the keyboard and below the range of the instrument articulations we will be key switching through. Change the Velocity from All to Unequal, and it will default to 0. The Conditions section should now look like what you see in Figure 26.4.

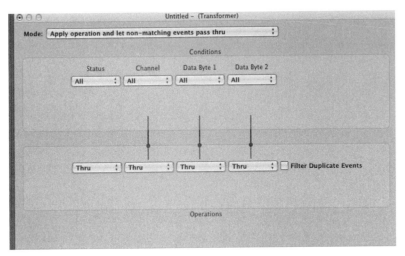

Figure 26.3   The default Transformer mode in the Environment window.

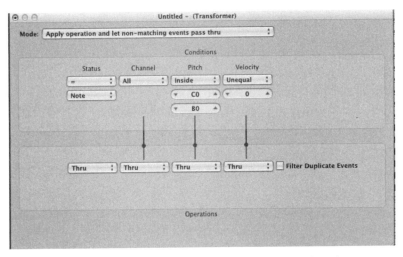

Figure 26.4   The Transformer's Conditions section completed.

5.   In the Transformer's Operations section change the Status from ALL to Fix, and once again a box will appear underneath it to select the kind of event that we want to alter. It will default to Fader, but hold down the mouse and change it to Program.

6.   Now change the Channel setting to Fix, and once again a box will appear underneath it, which defaults to 1. Click the right arrow, and it will change to 2, which is what we want. (Because Logic reserves MIDI channel 1 program changes for the channel strip, Kontakt needs to see MIDI channel 2 or above to change instrument banks in real time.) See Figure 26.5.

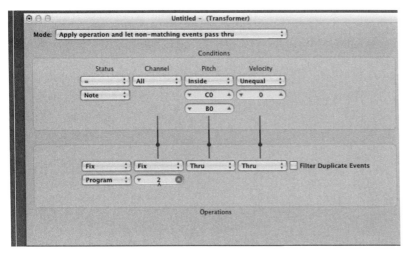

Figure 26.5   The Transformer's Operations section partially completed.

7.   You can leave Pitch set to Thru but change Velocity from Thru to Subtract, and once again, a box will appear underneath. Enter 24 into the box.

And here is why: You are setting up this Transformer to convert one type of MIDI message (note messages) into another type (program change messages). In MIDI-speak, the low note of our key-switching range, C0, is note number 24. But we need this to select the first program slot in Kontakt (#001), which corresponds to MIDI program change #0. So we get Logic to subtract 24 from the note number and plug the resulting number into a program change message to switch articulations in Kontakt! Here's how it works:

Key	MIDI Note #	Subtract 24 and You Get...	Resulting Program Change Value	Corresponding Kontakt Program Number
C0	24	0	0	001
C#0	25	1	1	002
D0	26	2	2	003
...	...	...	...	...
B0	31	11	11	012

8.   There is one more step of programming in the Transformer to perform. Because a note is a two-data-byte event and a program change is single-data-byte event, the Transformer needs to see this in the second data byte box, so the next step is necessary. Click on the dot in the last box twice so that it connects in the manner you see in Figure 26.6.

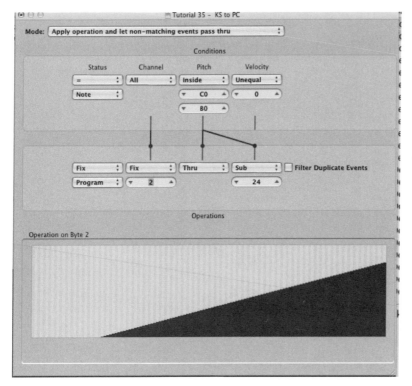

Figure 26.6   Connecting the dots in the Transformer's Operations section.

9.   In the last Operations box, change the setting from Through to Add and add -24, either by repeatedly clicking the left arrow or by double-clicking on 0 and typing in -24.

The Transformer setup is now complete! See Figure 26.7. Rename it if you like. I have chosen KS to PC.

Now it is time to hook this baby up! However, there may be times when we need those low notes to play notes for piano or contrabassoon, not trigger program changes, so first let's create a way to toggle this on and off.

10.   Under the New menu, navigate to Fader > Specials > Cable Switcher. See Figure 26.8.

11.   In the Inspector, set it to a range of from 0 to 1, as you see in Figure 26.9.

12.   Draw a cable from the top plug of the Physical Input (Sum) to the Cable Switcher and from the Cable Switcher plug to the Sequencer Input. Now a second plug appears. Cable it to the KS to PC Transformer. See Figure 26.10.

13.   Let's make it look a little more user friendly. In the Inspector, change the Cable Switcher's Style to Button 6, which has an ON button that you can toggle on or off. Toggle it on so it looks like Figure 26.11.

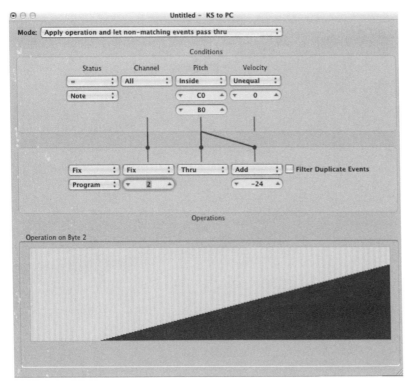

Figure 26.7   The Transformer setup for key switch to program changes.

14.   Now draw a cable from the top plug of the Transformer to the Input Notes Monitor, which is cabled to the Input View, which is cabled to the Sequencer Input. (As the two Input objects are really only ways of verifying that MIDI information is being passed, you could also bypass them and simply cable the Transformer to the Sequencer Input.) See Figure 26.12.

Arm the Kontakt 4 track, hit Record, and play and key switch to your heart's content. Further, if you create additional instrument banks in this Kontakt instance and load them with corresponding articulations from another violin section in LASS or even another library, they will all simultaneously change.

Okay, so in my example I want to play in a LASS Violin Legato part at Bar 1, switch to pizzicato at Bar 3, switch to tremolo at Bar 5, and end up with a trill at Bar 7. I do so, and you can see the magnificent work of art I have created in Figure 26.13. Obviously, I was a little late on the program changes, so in the Event List, I filter out the notes and controller data so that I am only viewing the program changes, and I quantize them to the bar by choosing 1/1. See Figure 26.14.

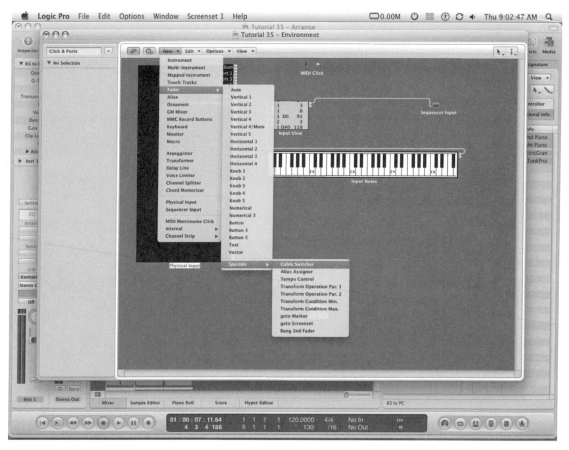

Figure 26.8   Creating the Cable Switcher.

I play back from the beginning, and it is perfect—all the articulations chase the program changes. However, if I want to play back from Bar 2, not only do I not hear legato, I do not hear anything. There are two issues.

In a new project, for some reason I cannot fathom, Logic defaults to not having notes chase. We need to change that.

1. In the Toolbar, choose Settings > MIDI.

2. Now click the Chase tab and notice that while Sustained is checked, Notes is not. Check it. See Figure 26.15.

   Now I go to Bar 2 and hit Play, and while it plays the whole note, it plays it as whatever articulation was triggered last, not legato. Remember that I mentioned that Logic reserves MIDI channel 1 for sending program changes to channel strips?

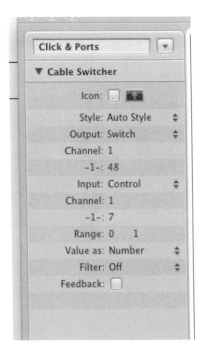

Figure 26.9   Setting the range for the Cable Switcher.

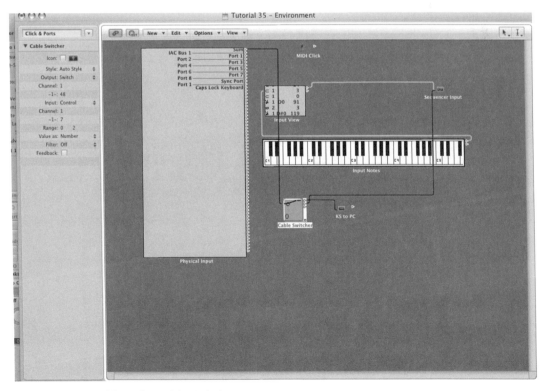

Figure 26.10   Cabling the Cable Switcher.

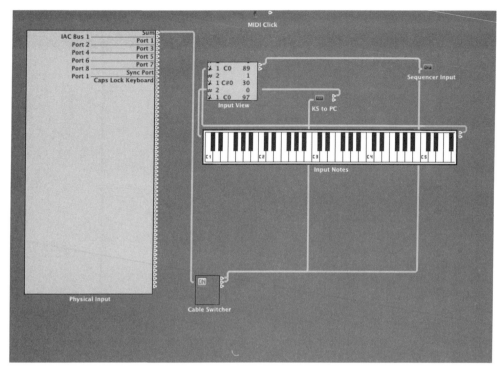

Figure 26.11   Changing the Cable Switcher from Auto Style to Button 6.

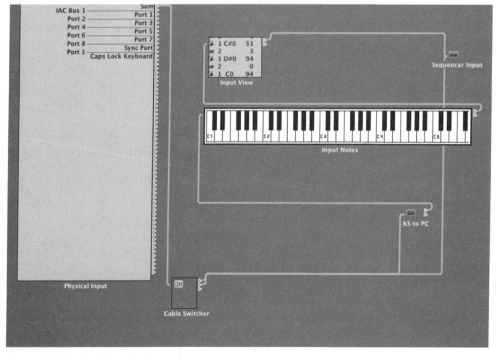

Figure 26.12   Cabling the Transformer.

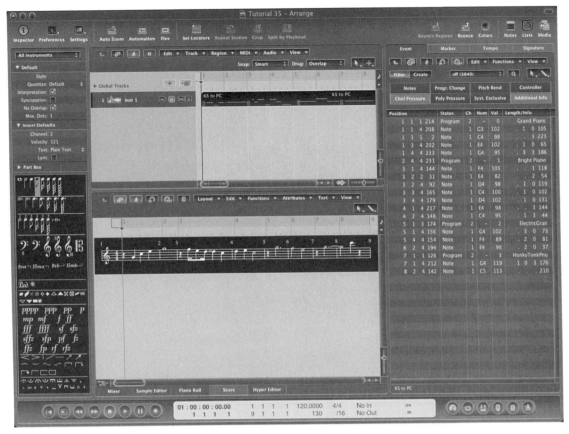

Figure 26.13 My violin part in the Score and Event List Editors.

3. In the filtered Event List, press Command+A to select all the program changes and change the MIDI channel (Ch) to 1.

Now when I play back from anywhere in the project, finally, my articulations chase perfectly!

Wow, that was a lot of work! However, you can now open up more K4 instances, create new instrument banks within them, and save them in a template, and you never have to do this again.

This will also work with Kontakt 4 or 3.5 loaded in Vienna Ensemble Pro exactly the same as if it were instantiated in Logic Pro 9.

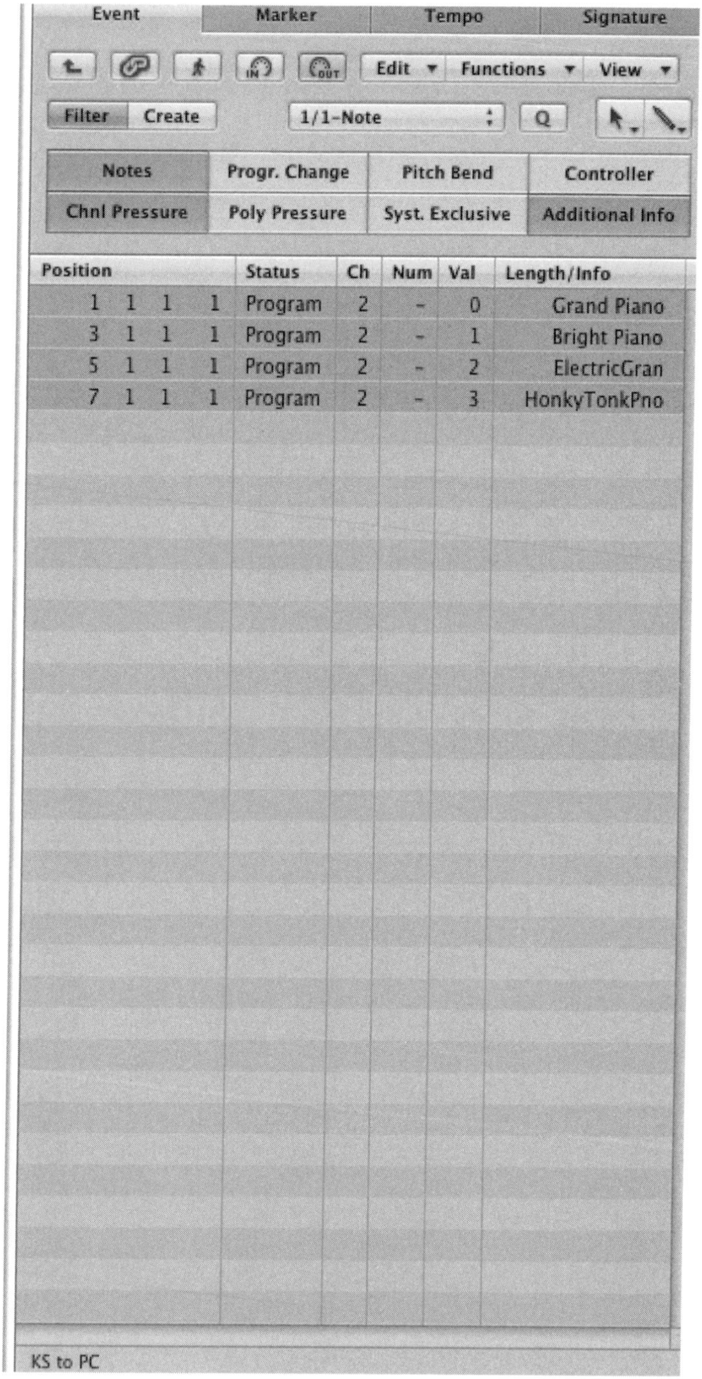

Figure 26.14 Quantized program changes in the Event List.

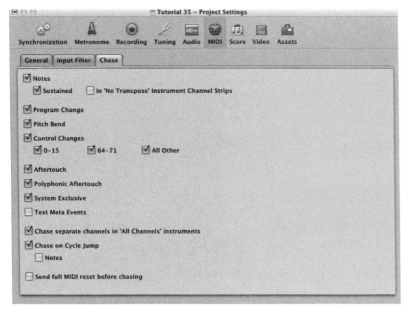

Figure 26.15   The Chase tab in the MIDI Project Settings.

Tutorial 27: Using Reason Version 4 via ReWire with Logic Pro 9

Propellerhead's Reason continues to be the "gateway drug" for many users that brings them to Logic Pro. And it is no wonder, as it brings a large number of sounds and beat-making capabilities, a sequencer, loops, arpeggios, and other tempo-dependent FX, all at a low price. Once again, I will assume you know your way around Reason reasonably well. (Pun intended.) (It should be mentioned that at the time I am writing this, Reason is not working properly with Logic Pro 9.1 when it is booted into 64-bit, but it is entirely possible that by the time you are reading this, the issues will have been resolved.)

Reason communicates with Logic Pro through ReWire, also an invention of Propellerhead. With Logic Pro 9, it is now really simple to get this puppy going. We have two setup needs:

1.   Send the MIDI to Reason so we can play and hear the MIDI parts.

2.   Bring the audio from Reason into Logic Pro to hear it and make it part of our mix.

Setting Up Logic Pro to Communicate with Reason

Logic Pro 9 must be launched first for Reason to communicate under ReWire. You will probably want to do this in a template, but here we will use a new project.

1.   Open LP9 and create a new project with one external MIDI instrument (not to be confused with the External instrument software instrument that is used in the Kontakt 3.5 tutorial).

2.   Open Reason, which now launches under ReWire.

3.   Create a Reason instrument, such as SubTractor, and a Mixer.

4.   Open the Mixer and click the plus sign on the left side of the page. When the dialog box opens, choose to create one or more new mono auxiliary channel strips, assigned to ascending inputs with the first being RW: Mix: L/R. (In actuality, this is ReWire 1/2.) See Figure 27.1.

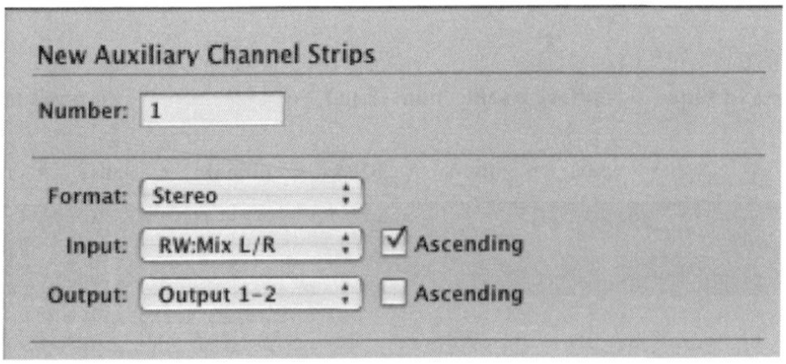

Figure 27.1   Auxiliary creation window in Logic Pro 9.

5. Click the Media button to open the Library and scroll down to the Reason folder. You will now see SubTractor 1 as a choice. Click it, and the General MIDI instrument you created becomes SubTractor 1 (see Figure 27.2). You can now record a MIDI region on this track.

Figure 27.2   Logic Pro 9's Arrange window with the Library view and a recorded MIDI region.

6. Open the Environment, navigate to the MIDI Instruments layer, and notice that LP9 created a ReWire MIDI instrument for Subtractor. See Figure 27.3.

7. Cycle the region, and in the Mixer, notice that the audio is being sent to Aux 1. See Figure 27.4.

Adding a Second Reason Instrument and Routing It into Logic Pro 9 Discretely

We will now add Reason's Thor Polysonic Synthesizer to our rig.

1. In Reason, add Thor and cable it to Audio Outputs 3 and 4 in the back of the Hardware Device (see Figure 27.5).

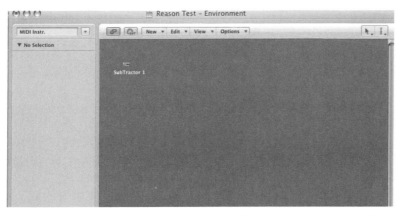

Figure 27.3   Environment layer with internal ReWire object created.

Figure 27.4   Logic's Mixer with Aux 1 receiving audio during playback of the MIDI region.

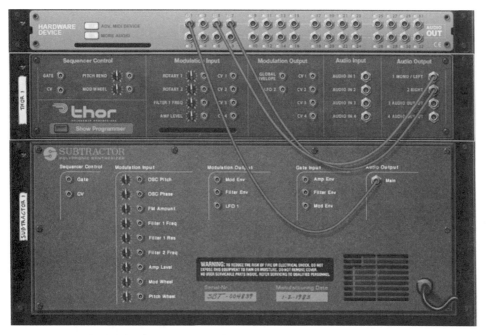

Figure 27.5   The back of Reason's Hardware Device with routed audio outputs.

2.   In Logic Pro, add another external MIDI instrument with the Library view of the Media area open and assign it to Thor.

3.   Record a MIDI region on the Thor track.

4.   Cycle and play back, and in the Mixer, notice that while Subtractor is still sending audio to Aux 1 (not also Aux 2, as it defaults to being a monophonic instrument), Thor is sending its audio to Auxes 3 and 4. See Figure 27.6.

Yes, it is this simple! You now have created a rack in Reason 4 that can receive discrete MIDI regions and play the Reason instruments while routing the audio back discretely into Logic Pro 9 through auxes.

> I highly recommend that you save the Reason Rack as a Reason song file and drag it into your Logic project folder if you have not bounced the tracks as audio, so that you have complete recallability without having to hunt for the Rack.

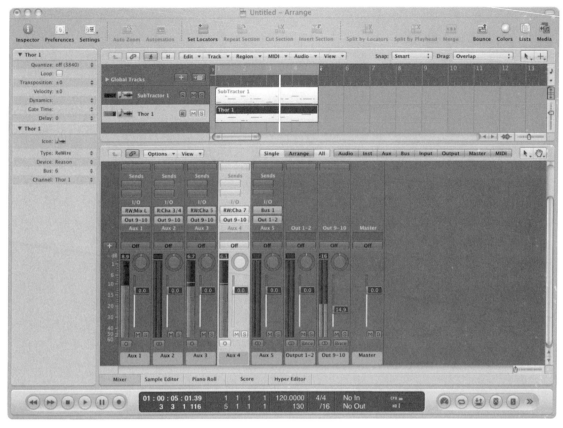

Figure 27.6   Logic Pro 9's Mixer with Auxes 1, 3, and 4 receiving audio during playback of the MIDI region.

Tutorial 28: Using ReCycle 2 with Logic Pro 9 and the EXS24

Propellerhead's ReCycle 2 is a favorite tool of loopmeisters, even in this era of Apple Loops. Its abilities to slice loops into REX files (.rx2) are very powerful. Once they are created, Logic Pro 9 has simple and flexible options for importing and using them.

While I assume that most of the users who will be interested in this tutorial are already experienced ReCycle users, I will nonetheless do some simple REX file creation here to entice those who are not.

Creating a REX 2 File in ReCycle 2

You can use any loop for this, whether it is a tempo-chasing loop, such as an ACID or Apple Loop, or one that is not. I am using a jungle beat that I downloaded from the Internet.

1. Open ReCycle, and it will prompt you to choose an audio file to open. See Figure 28.1.

2. Select the file, listen to it with Auto Play (or not), and open it.

3. ReCycle will ask you if you want to move the left locator to the first slice point. Click the Yes button.

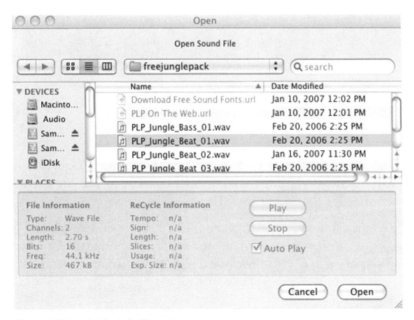

Figure 28.1 ReCycle's file selector.

4. It will then tell you that "to enable the effects, you must set the loop length and activate the Preview Toggle button on the top toolbar." Click OK.

5.   Under View, select Show Grid (Command+G), and it will tell you that the loop cannot be set to 0 bars. The loop I have chosen is clearly two bars long, so I type in 2.

6.   ReCycle will create what it thinks is the correct number of slices. By dragging the Sensitivity slider, you can add more or fewer. In my example, I am dragging it to the middle. See Figure 28.2.

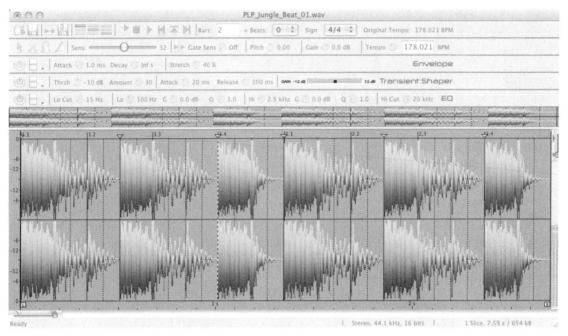

Figure 28.2   ReCycle's Sensitivity slider.

7.   Click on Preview Toggle to enable the FX. See Figure 28.3.

8.   The original calculated tempo was 178 bpm. I want it slower, so I double-click in the Tempo field and type 150. I wish it to be pitched a little higher, so I drag the Pitch up to 1.75. These tasks are performed in the area of the GUI you see in Figure 28.4.

9.   Just below it are the Envelope, Transient Shaper, and EQ FX. You can do many interesting things with these, especially if you know what you are doing. If not, there are some handy presets on the left side of each. For the Envelope, I have chosen Tighten Up, as you can see in Figure 28.5.

10.   I will choose Pressurize for the transient Shaper and Drum Cleanup for the EQ.

11.   I am now happy with this loop, so I choose Save As, and a dialog box comes up, allowing me to name it with the necessary extension .rx2.

12.   Quit ReCycle.

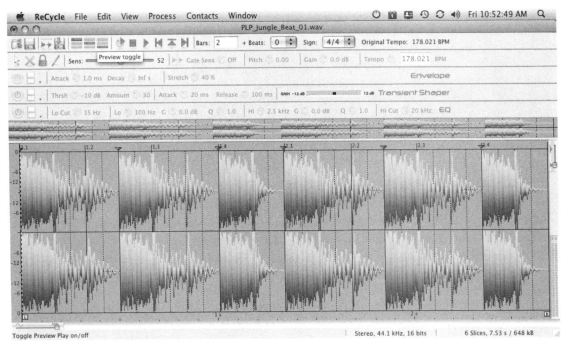

Figure 28.3   ReCycle's Preview Toggle button.

Figure 28.4   Changing tempo and pitch in ReCycle's GUI.

We have merely scratched the surface of what is possible in ReCycle, but this should get you going.

Bringing a REX 2 Loop onto an Audio Track in the Arrange Area

There are several easy ways to utilize your new loop in LP9. You can simply drag it onto an audio track.

1. Open a new empty project with one stereo audio track and one software instrument.

2. Locate the .rx2 loop and simply drag it onto the Audio 1 track in the Arrange area.

3. A dialog box will pop up. You want to choose Render into Apple Loop so that it will adjust to tempo changes. See Figure 28.6.

You now have many of the manipulating and editing capabilities of the .rx2 file that you have with an Apple Loop.

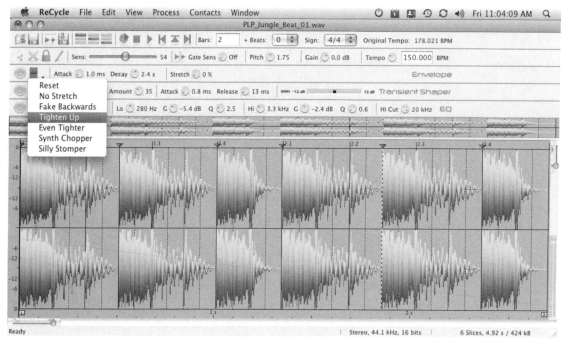

Figure 28.5   Tighten Up preset in the ReCycle Envelope.

Figure 28.6   The ReCycle File Import dialog box.

Bringing a REX 2 Loop into the EXS24

There are a couple of ways to use the .rx2 file in the EXS24. Here is the first method.

1.   Instantiate an EXS24 in the software instrument track you created, and the GUI will open up with no instrument selected. Do not load an instrument.

2.   Click on the Edit button to open the EXS24 Instrument Editor, which will obviously be empty. See Figure 28.7.

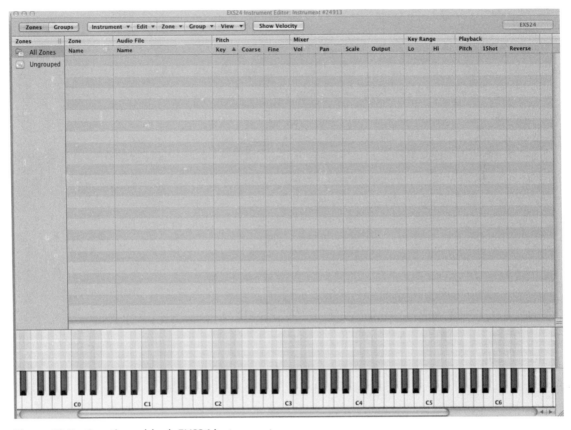

Figure 28.7   Creating a blank EXS24 instrument.

3.   Under the local Instrument menu, choose ReCycle Convert > Slice Loop and Make New Instrument. See Figure 28.8. The samples are loaded into the ESX24 Instrument Editor, and you now have a playable instrument, using the loop's sounds to create your own MIDI part. Be sure to save the EXS24 instrument.

4.   Alternatively, if you choose Extract MIDI Region and Make New Instrument, it will create the new EXS24 instrument as before, but also put the MIDI region on the track.

If you use both of these methods, you now have the best of all worlds: an Apple Loop, a playable EXS24 instrument, and a MIDI region that can play back using the EXS24 instrument created from the .rx2 loop.

Simple and powerful!

Figure 28.8   ReCycle converting in the EXS24 Instrument Editor.

Tutorial 29: Using Logic Pro 9 as a Software Instrument Rack for an Akai MPC3000

Many users come to Logic Pro 9 from hardware sequencers, lured by its powerful included array of software instruments. However, it does not necessarily mean that they want to abandon the machine that has a workflow and feel that they know and love, especially the Akai boxes with their idiosyncratic MIDI timing. By using Logic as a software instrument rack, they can have what is for them the best of both worlds.

In all probability, those of you who wish to go this route want to because you are already an MPC user, so for the purposes of this tutorial I will assume that you already know how to set it up and record MIDI data into it. I will be focusing on the Logic side of the equation.

Setting Up the Environment for an MPC3000 Template

1. Open a new empty project with 16 software instruments, as the MPC3000 supports 16 discrete MIDI channels.

2. Press Command+8 to open an Environment window and navigate to the layer named Clicks & Ports. See Figure 29.1.

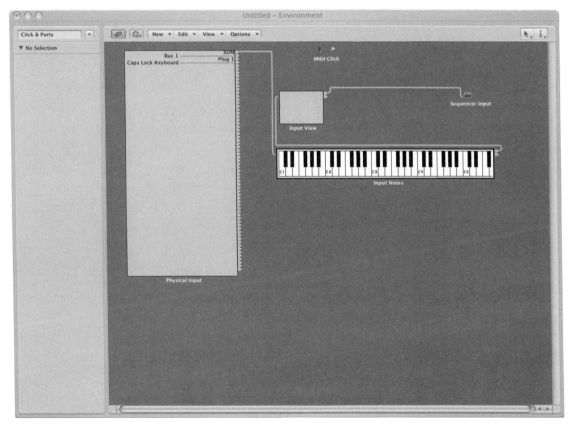

Figure 29.1   The Clicks & Ports Environment layer.

3. Rubber-band over all the objects in the layer, and under the local Edit menu, choose Clear Cables Only.

    Although you eventually probably want to put much of what you will now create on its own layer, it is easier to create and cable the objects on this later.

4. Under the local New menu, create a new multi instrument. Use the Text tool to rename it, perhaps MPC.

5. Click on each of the subchannels in the MPC multi instrument to enable them. The lines going through them will disappear to reflect this status. You may want to move one of the objects that you are not using out of the way a little bit before you do the next step.

6. Draw a cable from the MIDI port on the physical input that represents the port on your MIDI interface that your MPC3000 is patched into—in this example, Port 1—to the newly created MPC instrument.

7. Under the New menu, create a channel splitter and draw a cable to it from the MPC multi instrument. See Figure 29.2.

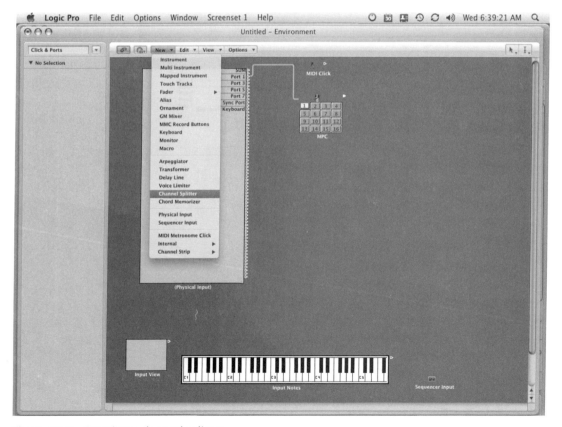

Figure 29.2 Creating a channel splitter.

A dialog box will appear, asking whether you want to remove the channels port setting. Click No. See Figure 29.3.

Figure 29.3   The Channel Port Settings dialog box.

Everything you need has now been created, but some cabling tasks remain. For the sake of ergonomics, let's keep them on the same Environment layer.

Now comes some mildly tedious but necessary work. You might find it helpful if your eyesight is less than stellar to temporarily change your monitor's screen resolution to something a little larger.

8. Draw a cable from each of the 16 MIDI channels in the channel splitter to each of the software instruments. Make sure you do not have two cables going to one software instrument. See Figure 29.4.

9. Load in the software instruments you wish to use. Let's move them to the Mixer layer, where they more logically belong. (Or you could create a new layer.)

Figure 29.4 Cabling from the channel splitter to the software instruments.

10.   Shift-select the MPC multi instrument and the channel splitter. While holding down the Option key, click and hold on the top-left pop-up menu and navigate to the Mixer layer, and the two objects will be moved to that layer. (Don't worry about cabling between layers. The cabling from the physical input to the MPC multi instrument is preserved.)

11.   Move them around on the layer so they are not superimposed on the software instrument channel strips. See Figure 29.5.

12.   Save as a template.

Logic Pro 9 now has a properly set-up template to function as a software instrument rack for the MPC3000. Remember that since you are recording into the MPC, not Logic itself, selecting tracks in the Arrange window will not determine what you hear when you play your controllers, but the track selection in the MPC3000. So simply select the track with the MIDI channel assignment you wish to play, hear, and subsequently record, and you are rolling!

Figure 29.5 Software instruments loaded in the Mixer Environment layer.

Troubleshooting

If, when you select a track with a proper MIDI channel assignment in the MPC3000 and you play your controller, you do not hear the expected Logic software instrument, there are a few things you can check.

1.   Is the port assignment for the MPC3000 in the Logic Environment correct when you select the MPC multi instrument?

2.   Is the cabling from the channel splitter correct?

3.   Is the MPC3000 properly cabled to the MIDI interface?

4.   The MPC3000 software defaults to settings you need unless the user changes them. Nonetheless, if you have no other explanation for why things are not working properly, choose the MPC's MIDI menu and press 2. Make sure the MPC is still set to:

     a. Receive: All

     b. Local: On

     c. Soft Thru: On

Tutorial 30: Creating and Placing 2 Pops in Logic Pro 9 Projects for Audio File Alignment in a Pro Tools Session

Those of us who compose to picture remember the days, not so long ago, when the preferred delivery method of post houses required all our music to be recorded as stems or stereo mixes onto tape on a digital multitrack tape recorder, such as the Tascam DA-88. This required our DAW of choice to be synced to the DA-88 with enough pre-roll for the DA-88 to see a burst of time code to chase. With no intended disrespect to Tascam, I do not miss those days.

Nowadays, we are mostly asked to deliver our mixes and stems in Pro Tools sessions. Although we could simply put the audio files into protocols at the SMPTE start times for each cue, to be dead certain that the picture mixer has them exactly at the right placement in Pro Tools, it is a good idea to create a pop that is placed at two seconds before the cue begins. This is commonly referred to as a *2 Pop*.

Recording and Placing the 2 Pop

For the purposes of this tutorial, if you have not already done so, convert all the software instrument tracks to audio files. This is now easier than ever in Logic Pro 9, thanks to the long-requested Bounce Track in Place and Bounce-Replace All Tracks features, as well as exporting them.

1. Suppose the music you have composed for your cue—let's call it 1M4—enters at 01:08:36:00 at a frame rate of 29.97 fps. Its tempo begins at a quarter note and equals 136 bpm, and the meter is 4/4. You have set the project's beginning to 01:08:36:00 and adjusted the movie start so that at Bar 1 1 1 1, SMPTE time is what you see in both Logic Pro's SMPTE display and the burn window of your movie. See Figure 30.1.

2. In the Event List, under the local View menu, select Event Position and Length in SMPTE Units.

3. Select all the audio regions and lock them to SMPTE position to ensure that they do not get moved accidentally.

4. Drag the project start marker back a couple of bars, for example, to −2 1 1 1. Don't be concerned if you see a different meter, because what you are doing next is totally about SMPTE position, and therefore the meter display is irrelevant.

5. Use the Go to Position key command, and in the As SMPTE area, double-click where it says 36 in the third field (the seconds field) and type in 34 to place the 2-pop two seconds before the start of the cue. Click OK.

6. Use the Go to Position key command again. Thankfully, it remembers your last entry.

7. Create a new software instrument and open a blank EXS24. It defaults to a sine wave, which is fine for a 2 Pop.

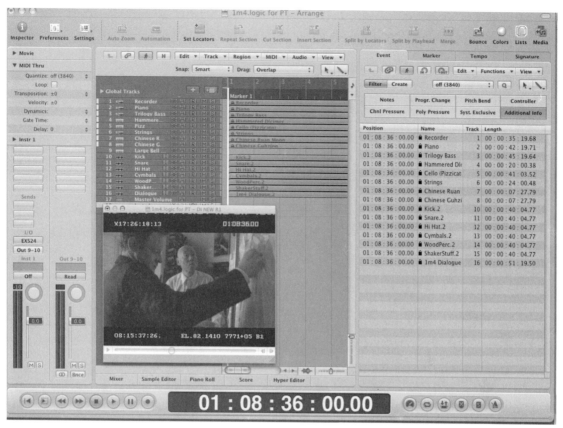

Figure 30.1   A Logic Pro 9 Arrange window with SMPTE time in the Transport, matching the burn window on the proxy movie.

8. Create a new MIDI region with the Pencil tool and name it 2 Pop. You do not need to be precise as to its location, because you will now use the key command for Pickup Clock to place it precisely at the correct position. Hit the Go to Position key command once again to ensure that the playhead is at the precise SMPTE position you need, then hit the key command for Pickup Clock, which moves the event to the playhead position.

9. Open the EXS24 region in the editor of your choice and insert a note. I suggest B5 for a 2 Pop. Make sure that the note is exactly at the correct SMPTE position and adjust the length. I prefer to use the Event List for this, because it is the most precise. I like my 2 Pop to be two frames in length. Some people like one frame. I also like to set the volume to be between –10 and –20 dB.

10. Select the EXS24 region, and in the Toolbar, click the Set Locators button to create a bounce range. It is now ready to be bounced to an audio file, as you can see in Figure 30.2.

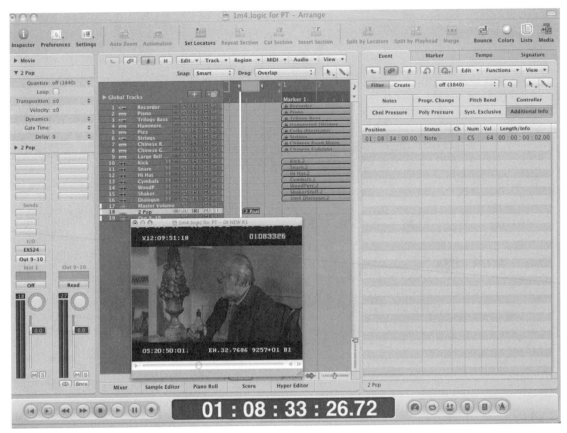

Figure 30.2   In this figure, the project start has been adjusted, and an EXS24 2 Pop is ready to be bounced.

11. Solo the EXS24 and bounce it to create an audio file of the 2 Pop with the check box for adding it to the Audio Bin selected.

12. Turn off the cycle, un-solo the EXS24, and delete the EXS24 MIDI region.

13. Drag the 2-Pop audio region from the Audio Bin to the Arrange window below the existing tracks, and LP9 will create the next available audio track to play it. Use the Go to Position and Pickup Clock key commands to ensure the region is in the right place and then lock the region to SMPTE.

14. Select all the regions, and then in the Toolbar, choose Set Locators. Bounce to a stereo mix, which now will begin with the 2 Pop at 01:08:34:00. See Figure 30.3. (If you are creating stems, you could copy the 2 Pop to every track to be super-safe and bounce or export them.)

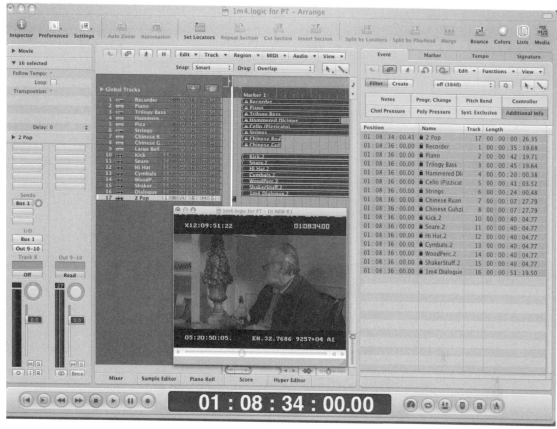

Figure 30.3   The Arrange window and the Event List with all the audio files/regions in their proper places, ready to be bounced to a stereo mix.

You will no doubt want to save the 2-pop bounce to some place on your hard drive where you can easily find it whenever you need it.

The files are now ready to be placed in a Pro Tools session.

Placing the Audio Files in a Pro Tools Session (for Delivery to Post-Production)

If you are a tad forgetful, like me, you now probably should write down your SMPTE start time. We will now add a stereo mix with the 2 Pop to a Pro Tools session. This requires a version of Pro Tools that has the time code option.

1.   Open Pro Tools and create a new session. For this example, name it Reel 1.

2.   Under the Setup window, choose Session and set the start time to 00:58:30:00 to allow for the 2 Pop and some pre-roll. Make sure that the frame rate is correct—in this case, 29.97 fps Non-Drop. See Figure 30.4.

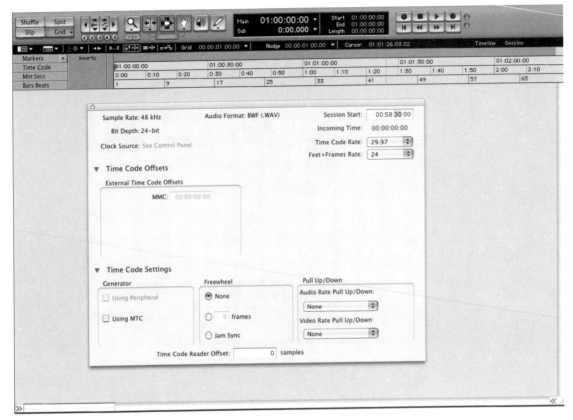

Figure 30.4 A Pro Tools Session Setup window.

3.   In the upper left of the Pro Tools Edit window, choose the Spot Mode button.

4.   From the Finder, drag the stereo mix (or stems) with the included 2 Pop(s) into the blank area of the Edit window. A dialog box pops up, allowing you to type in the location. In this example you would enter 01:08:34:00. See Figure 30.5.

Pro Tools creates the necessary audio track(s) and places the audio file(s) at the proper SMPTE time code position. See Figure 30.6.

Your audio files, including the 2 Pop, are now placed properly in your Pro Tools session on your way to creating a Pro Tools session for the first reel for delivery.

Repeat the processes for all remaining cues in Reel 1 and then do the same for subsequent reels. Your delivery will be bulletproof, and you will have established yourself in the picture mixer's eyes as a pro!

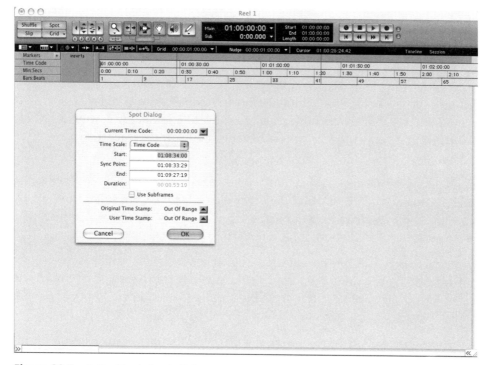

Figure 30.5   A Pro Tools Spot dialog.

Figure 30.6   A stereo mix with a 2 Pop properly placed in the Pro Tools session.

Tutorial 31: Using Vienna Ensemble Pro with Logic Pro 9 on the Same Computer

In the last few years, things have changed dramatically for those composers who are trying to do orchestral mockups and/or run many large sample-based libraries and software instruments on the Mac in applications such as Logic Pro, Digital Performer, Cubase, and even Pro Tools. With today's powerful Intel Macs, CPU power is not really as much of an issue. Accessing RAM has been the new major bottleneck, as today's sample libraries and software instruments are frequently very RAM hungry.

While the newer computers are 64-bit capable, and Apple's OS X 10.6 (Snow Leopard) is also fully 64-bit capable, because Logic Pro 9.0 and the other major DAWs were still 32-bit, we are limited by the fact that 32-bit apps can load at most 4 GB of RAM in theory, and in fact, with Logic Pro 9.0, if you get above 3.5 GB used, it becomes rather unstable.

Since I initially wrote this tutorial, Apple has released Logic Pro 9.1, which is indeed 64-bit capable. However, at the time I am writing this, most of the popular third-party software instruments are not yet 64-bit, so they are hosted in a 32-bit "bridge" when Logic Pro 9.1 is in 64-bit mode.

While Apple and Native Instruments have done some clever programming to allow both the EXS24 and Kontakt 3.5/4 to address more RAM in memory pools outside of Logic, with Kontakt in particular it uses Logic's Virtual Memory, and eventually you hit a wall. To work around this issue, users have been running some software instruments in standalone mode or in a host such as Plogue Bidule, and while this works, it requires ReWire or some other MIDI routing and or third-party software for audio, such as Soundflower, or audio interface ADAT Lightpipe routing, both of which have some disadvantages. This will not change until all or most of the other popular third-party software instruments become 64-bit.

Enter Vienna Instruments! (Ta DA!) The folks at Vienna have enabled their Ensemble to host third-party Audio Units on the same computer, or on another computer, with no additional MIDI apps or audio routing necessary. (This requires a USB key distributed by Steinberg.) Even with the release of a 64-bit version of Logic Pro, this is an important application, as it allows you to use more 32-bit software instruments than with Logic Pro only and spares you waiting for long reload times for software instruments when changing Logic Pro 9 projects. This is particularly helpful for film/TV work, where it is common to have many cues that use essentially the same palette.

Logic Pro 9 communicates best with Vienna Ensemble Pro by connecting to server apps, both 64-bit and 32-bit. You start these servers on every computer that you wish to connect to Logic Pro 9. While Vienna Instruments itself and Stylus RMX are 64-bit and more will be coming, for now others can be loaded in the 32-bit server, in which you can run eight instances of 16 MIDI channels each, with no discernable latency. (You can run more MIDI channels using IAC busses, but IMHO the latency becomes unacceptable.)

I will not be going much into the Vienna Instruments software instrument, as they have terrific video tutorials available, but instead I'll focus on integrating VE Pro with Logic Pro 9. For now, we will work with the 32-bit server, as there are so many more Audio Units we can run in it, and the methodology is the same.

Connecting Logic Pro 9 to the VE Pro 32-Bit Server

While not technically necessary, I recommend that you open the server before you open Logic Pro 9, as it is a little simpler and in my experience seems to be more reliable. In your Vienna Ensemble Pro folder, you will find both the Vienna Ensemble Pro Server (64-bit) and one named simply the Vienna Ensemble Pro Server, which is the 32-bit server. Add the 32-bit server to the Dock. Click on the 32-bit server icon to open it and place it on your screen where you like. See Figure 31.1.

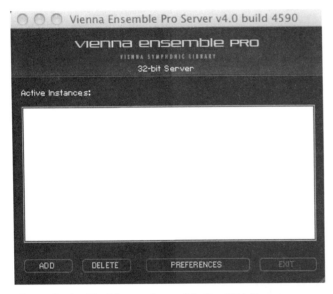

Figure 31.1   The Vienna Ensemble Pro 32-bit server.

Now we are ready to open Logic and create a new empty project with a software instrument. Unlike Logic Pro 9, VE Pro handles multi-timbral instances quite well, so we will be using them.

1. Open a new empty project with a multi-timbral software instrument with 16 MIDI channels.

2. Open the Mixer and in the software instrument's I/O, instantiate a multi-output instance of VE Pro. A sever interface window will pop up. See Figure 31.2.

3. Notice the two rectangles, one labeled Decouple and the other Connect. If you do not click on Decouple, the VE Pro instance will not be linked to your Logic project when you open it at a later date and will recall the plug-in data. While this is really useful for

Figure 31.2 The VE Pro server interface.

recallability, it negates the advantage of avoiding long reloading times. Each choice has its advantages. For now, we will not decouple.

4. Click on the rectangle where it says Connect, and you will see the 32-bit server listed under Available Slaves, as you see in Figure 31.3. Choose the 32-bit server and click Connect. Click on its icon in the Dock, and you can see that VE Pro opens a 32-bit instance with a Vienna Ensemble instrument and a master bus created by default. See Figure 31.4.

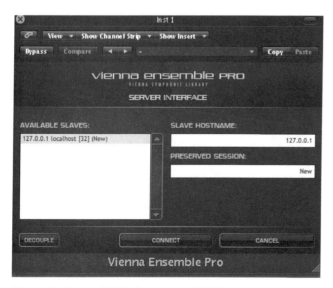

Figure 31.3 Available instances of VE Pro server.

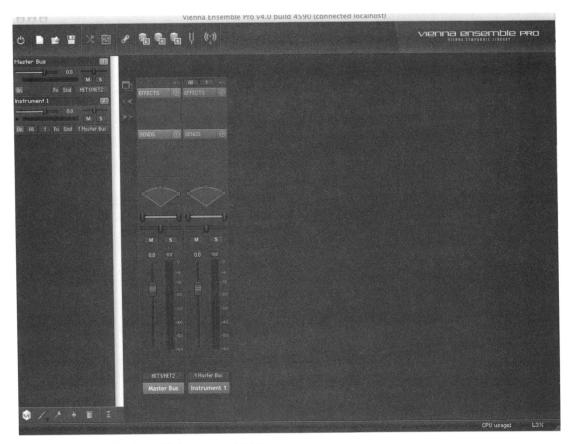

Figure 31.4 A default 32-bit instance of VE Pro.

5. Double click on Instrument 1, and it will open up the interface. By double-clicking the preset, I will use the Appassionata Strings that come as part of the Epic Orchestra instruments that the nice Vienna folks are including with the purchase of VE Pro at this time.

6. Click the Matrix Assign tab, and you will see 01 App Strings-Matrix. Double-click on it, and it will load the Matrix. See Figure 31.5.

7. Click the Patch Assign tab cells 1A–6A, each of which has a different articulation loaded, as you see in Figure 31.6. You can navigate between them through many different controllers, such as the mod wheel or key switches, which is explained well in the Vienna Ensemble video tutorials. Also, when in Record mode in LP9, you can simply click on the cells to change articulations.

8. Toggle back to the Mixer view by hitting the Esc key on your keyboard. In the upper-left of the Mixer, rename Instrument 1 by double-clicking on the name and typing in Vienna Strings. Let's assign this instrument's output to bring it in discretely in LP9.

Figure 31.5 The Matrix Assign tab in a Vienna Ensemble Instrument.

9. In the Mixer section of VE Pro, directly to the right of the word On, are two MIDI assignment boxes. Hold down the mouse and change the first one from All to 1 plug in MIDI in 1 and set the second box to MIDI channel 1. See Figure 31.7.

10. Right above the name in the rectangle you see that lists Master Bus, hold down the mouse and choose Net/3/4. This will route it to the first aux we create for the Vienna Ensemble Pro multi-output software instrument in LP9. See Figure 31.8.

11. Return to Logic's Mixer in Single view and click the plus sign on the Instrument 1 channel strip. LP9 will create an aux with the properly assigned input. Play your keyboard, and you will hear the sound and notice that it is coming in on Aux 1, which you can now rename Vienna Strings, if you'd like. You can also rename Instrument 1 VE Pro 1, as I have done. You will see what appears here in Figure 31.9.

    We will now begin to add Audio Units and create inputs for them in VE Pro and corresponding auxes in LP9, but first we want to "preserve" this 32-bit instance so if we change projects this is still available to us.

Figure 31.6   The Patch Assign tab in a Vienna Ensemble Instrument

12.   In the toolbar at the top of the Vienna instrument GUI is an icon that is hard to describe but is directly to the right of the tuning fork icon. See Figure 31.10. Click it to name and preserve the instance.

Adding Additional AUs to the Vienna Ensemble Pro Instance and Connecting Them with Logic Pro 9

As I said, presently we are limited to 16 discrete MIDI channels per instance with Logic Pro 9, but we can have up to 8 instances through one 32-bit server. Since we are only addressing one MIDI channel so far in this preserved instance, let's add some more.

1.   In VE Pro, hit Command+V, and a menu of your Audio Units appears from which to choose. I am choosing Kontakt 4.

2.   As I did with the Vienna Strings, I now rename the K4 multi to what I intend to load—in this case, Ruby Winds—and assign its MIDI channels to All.

Figure 31.7   A Vienna Strings instrument renamed with MIDI set to the proper MIDI plug-in and assigned to a discrete output.

3.   The GUI opens, and I now will use Kontakt 4's wonderful new Quick-Load feature to load in a Kirk Hunter Ruby Woodwinds Multi I have previously created. Notice that the output assignments start with Stereo 2, as Stereo 1 routes to the whole K4 AU, and the MIDI channels start with A2, as A1 is being used by the Vienna Strings. See Figure 31.11.

4.   I hit Command+I seven times to create seven inputs. In the rectangles where it says No Input, I assign the input to Ruby Winds 2, the next input to 3, then next input to 4, and so on. Using the same method, I now assign the Inputs outputs to Net 5/6, Net 7/8, and so on. The instance should now appear as in Figure 31.12.

Figure 31.8   The Vienna Strings instrument assigned to a discrete output.

Figure 31.9   A Vienna instrument and an aux in LP9's Mixer with Single view.

Figure 31.10   The Preserve Instance icon to the right of the Master Tuning icon in VE Pro.

At this point you will want to preserve the instance again to update its configuration. We still have six MIDI channels available for this instance, but for the sake of trying to keep this tutorial from getting too long, we will move on to another instance. (You also may want to save this VE Pro project.)

Setting Up AUs in Another Instance and Connecting Them with Logic Pro 9

In this instance, we will add a couple of RAM-hungry but amazing-sounding beasts, Spectrasonics' Omnisphere and Trillian. (Yeah, I am an unabashed fanboy. By the time you read this, however, you will be able to load them in the 64-bit server. The procedures will be the same.)

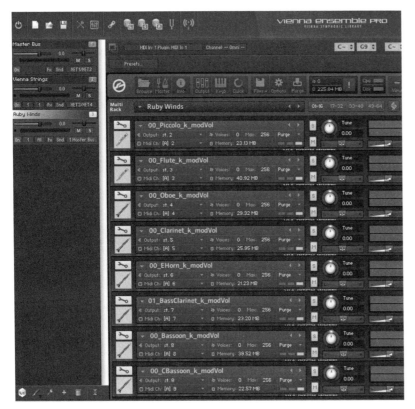

Figure 31.11 The Kontakt 4 multi with MIDI and output assignments.

1. In the VE Pro 32-bit server, *not* the instance under the File menu, click Add. It will ask you to name the new instance, and when you do and click OK, VE Pro will open a new instance with the expected default configuration. As before, delete Instrument 1 and add an Audio Unit. Load in Omnisphere.

2. Click on the tab called Multi, which will obviously be empty. From the menu, load in a multi such as Back to the Middle Ages Split. Click on the Mixer tab. Notice that it loads in Stack mode. Click on the Stack tab, and you will see a lit power button next to Stack mode. Turn it off and return to the Mixer tab. Notice that the multi has loaded three patches assigned to MIDI channels 1–3, all going to Output A. Assign the sounds to Outs B, C, and D. See Figure 31.13.

3. Using the method we did in the other instance, create three inputs in VE Pro and assign their inputs and outputs accordingly, as in Figure 31.14.

4. Preserve the instance and name it, such as Synth Rack.

5. Back in Logic Pro, create a new multi-timbral software instrument with three MIDI channels, load in a multi-output VE Pro, and connect to this Synth Rack instance.

Figure 31.12　The VE Pro instance configured.

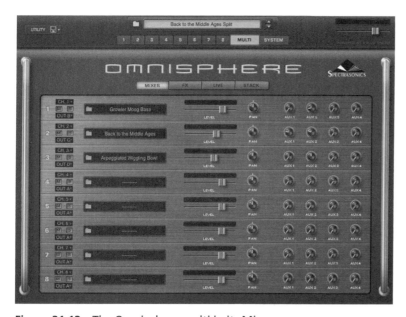

Figure 31.13　The Omnisphere multi in its Mixer page.

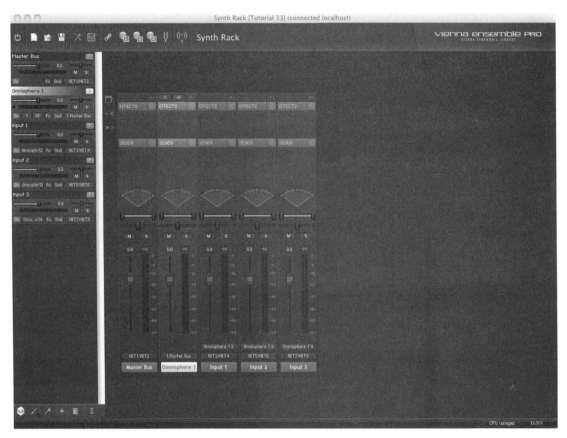

Figure 31.14 Omnisphere's inputs configured in a second VE Pro instance.

6. As before, create three auxes to receive the inputs from VE Pro, and it is all good to go.

    Let's add an acoustic bass, à la Wyclef Jean. We will use Spectasonics' amazing new Trillian. If you have forgotten how to do any of what follows, refer to the text and figures used in the creation of the first instance.

7. As we did in the other instance, we will add the Audio Unit, open a patch such as Trillian Acoustic 1,and assign its MIDI channel to the next available, which is MIDI channel 4.

8. Because it is only one sound, we do not need to create another VE Pro input, but merely assign the output of Trillian to NET 9/10.

9. Back in Logic, use the key command Option+Command+M to create the next MIDI channel track, and in the Mixer, click the plus sign for the instrument to create one more aux.

We still have 10 more MIDI channels available to use in this instance and six more instances we can create, all using the one Vienna Ensemble Pro 32-bit server. No doubt, over the coming months we will see more and more software instruments become 64-bit capable on the Mac and then, with VE Pro's 64-bit server, the sky is the limit!

Linking VE Pro on a second computer to Logic Pro 9 by connecting the two computers with an Ethernet cable (both must have gigabit Ethernet) involves exactly the same procedures. Bear in mind that you will need a Syncrosoft key for each computer you want VE Pro to run on and that if your second computer is a PC, you will need VST rather than AU versions of the software instruments.

Power User Tip: If in Logic Pro 9 you save the Vienna Ensemble Pro instance as a channel strip setting, when you call it up in any Logic Pro 9 project, it will load VE Pro with the same software instruments, complete with inputs and their I/O assignments. The only things you will have to re-create are Logic's auxes to receive the VE Pro inputs, which, as you know, you can literally do in seconds. It does, however, seem to have an undefined size limitation.

Tutorial 32: Using Plogue Bidule with Logic Pro 9 on the Same Computer

In my earlier tutorial on Vienna Ensemble Pro, I was fairly specific about the advantages of it over Plogue Bidule as a secondary software instrument host . So why this tutorial?

There are several reasons why you might still want to use Plogue Bidule instead of (or in addition to, as I am doing) VE Pro.

- It is not a new product, but tried and true, and it does lots of other neat MIDI things, audio processing and routing, FX, and so on that we will not be covering in this tutorial.

- It is very inexpensive and allows you to use it in demo mode fully featured for free for quite a while, so you have ample time to see how well it works for you.

- You like its patchbay-style interface, similar to Logic's Environment.

- You are Canadian, and you wish to support your countryman, Sebastien Beaulieu, who developed this.

Considerations

There are several methods for connecting Plogue Bidule's audio and MIDI to LP9. The most obvious is ReWire, and it is attractive because the MIDI timing is impeccable and no additional audio interface/application is necessary. But there is one flaw that is a deal-breaker for me. All the software instruments loaded in Plogue Bidule under ReWire will be addressed by only one core of your Mac. This is not Plogue Bidule's fault; it is a ReWire limitation.

One choice is to use an application such as Soundflower or Jack OS, or to use routing in your audio interface if it has ADAT Lightpipe I/O. In my tutorial on using Kontakt as a standalone, I have already described the necessary work for Soundflower, so I will not reiterate it here.

A better solution because it is simpler and more direct anyway is to use ADAT Lightpipe I/O if your audio interface has that capability, and many, if not most, nowadays do. Some require actually physical patching of cables from outs to ins, while others can do it in their software that they supply. However, since I cannot assume that you have an audio interface with this capability, I will use Soundflower again.

Setting Up Plogue Bidule

You need to open Plogue Bidule before you open Logic Pro 9, so that it will not open in ReWire mode.

1. From your Applications folder, navigate to the Plogue Bidule folder, and then in the Layouts folder within it, double-click on the layout named default.bidule. It will look roughly like what you see in Figure 32.l.

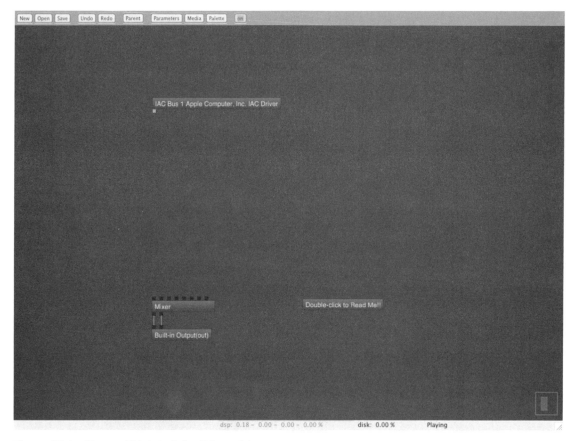

Figure 32.1 Plogue Bidule's default template.

2.   You can drag and reposition the objects around the GUI with your mouse. You can also resize them and move them in the little brown square within a square in the lower-right corner, although personally I find this hard to control and prefer assigning the right button of my trackball to zoom in and out.

3.   While we could use the existing objects as a jumping-off point, let's build this puppy from scratch. Use Command+A to select all and hit Delete.

4.   Under the Plogue Bidule menu in the Finder, choose Preferences. In the User Interface tab, you can choose a skin, curve style, and so on. I am using one called Sonshi, which is a free downloadable skin, but let us choose the default and click Apply. See Figure 32.2.

5.   Unfortunately, this closes the Preferences window, so now we must open it again. Navigate to the ReWire tab and make sure that Enable ReWire Mixer is not checked.

6.   Navigate to the DSP tab and choose the sample rate you will be working with in LP9. The default buffer size will be 256. You may be able to use a lower buffer size, which will give

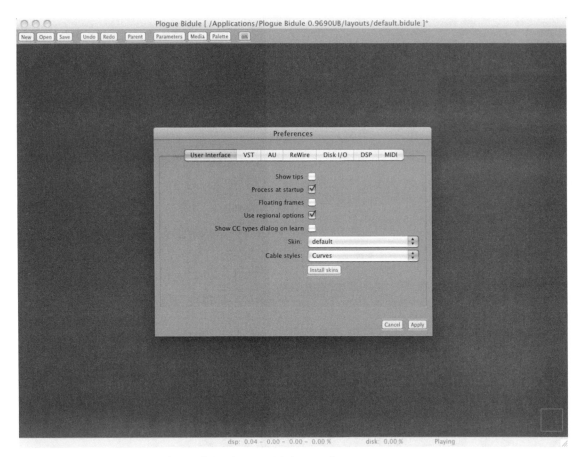

Figure 32.2   The User Interface tab in Plogue Bidule's Preferences.

you less latency depending on how many software instruments you load in and how demanding they are of your computer's resources, but for now, let us leave it at the default.

7.   Navigate to the MIDI tab, set the number of virtual MIDI ports to 16, and check Reduce MIDI Jitter, as you see in Figure 32.3. Click Apply.

It is now time to populate our Plogue Bidule instance. At the top left of the GUI is a toolbar with tabs. We will be concerning ourselves with the two most to the right that read Palette and On. Obviously, we want the On/Off button to read On.

1.   Click the Palette tab, and a menu will open to the left. See Figure 32.4.

2.   The first thing we need to create is an audio device. Open the disclosure arrows for Audio Devices > Output, and you will see your available choices. Choose Soundflower (16ch) (out) and drag it into the GUI. Plogue Bidule should now look like Figure 32.5.

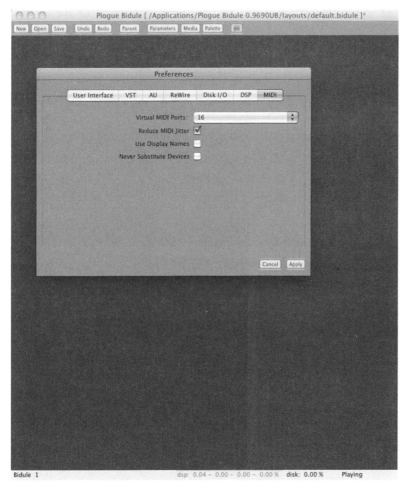

Figure 32.3   The MIDI tab in Plogue Bidule's Preferences.

3.   Close the disclosure triangles in the palette and open the disclosure triangles for MIDI Devices > Input. Here, among your choices, you will see 16 Bidule MIDI inputs. These are internal MIDI busses created by Plogue Bidule itself. For now, let us drag Bidule 1 and Bidule 2 into the GUI. See Figure 32.6.

Let's add a software instrument. From the palette, open the disclosure triangle for AU Music Devices and navigate to the folder for the developer of one of yours. I will be using Spectrasonics Omnisphere. As before, I simply drag it into the GUI.

1.   On the Omnisphere object, you will see a square for MIDI cabling out on the top and 16 of them for outputs on the bottom. Draw a cable from the top square to the Bidule 1 MIDI input.

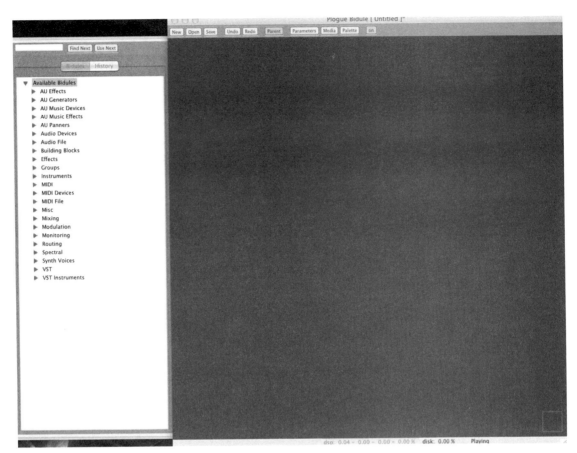

Figure 32.4   Plogue Bidule with an open palette.

2.   It is my intention to load two patches into Omnisphere assigned to two different MIDI channels and two separate stereo outputs, so one by one, draw cables from the first four outs from the Omnisphere object to the first four ins on the Soundflower object. This will give you the desired two stereo outputs. Plogue Bidule should now look like Figure 32.7.

Actually, you can cable all the outputs at one time by holding down the Command key or the Shift key while you draw the first cable, but since that would be more outputs than I want to use, I did not do so. I would then simply load two patches into Omnisphere's Mixer, one assigned to MIDI channel 1 and Output A and the other assigned to MIDI channel 2 and Output B. I am using one choir and one strings patch.

Let's add another software instrument. Follow the previously described procedure and drag in another. I will use Sample Logic's unique Morphestra library, which uses the Kontakt 3 Player,

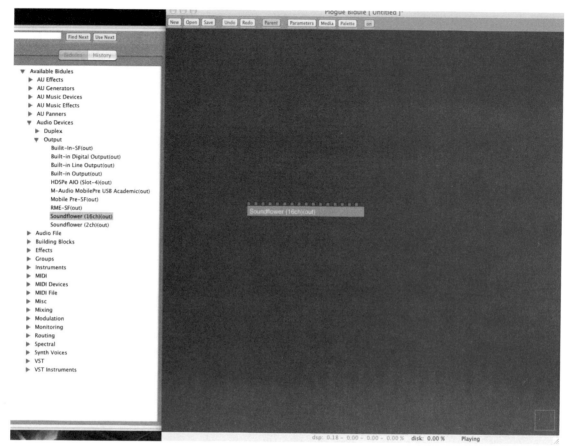

Figure 32.5 Plogue Bidule with the Soundflower audio device.

but you may use any one you choose. I will actually be loading it into the full version of Kontakt 4, since that gives me greater flexibility than the player.

1. Notice that Kontakt 4 gives you a choice of how many outputs you want to create it with, as do Play and some others. It is my intention to load three patches from Morphestra discretely, so I will choose 00 ins 06 outs and drag it in. This will give me three stereo outputs.

2. As before, I cable to another MIDI input, Bidule 2.

3. Holding down the Command key, I can now simultaneously cable the six outputs from K4 to the next six inputs in Soundflower. So now Plogue Bidule should look like Figure 32.8.

4. I double-click on the Kontakt 4 object, and the GUI opens. Because Morphestra is a Kontakt Player–based library, it shows up in the Libraries tab on the left, so I do not have to use the Browser.

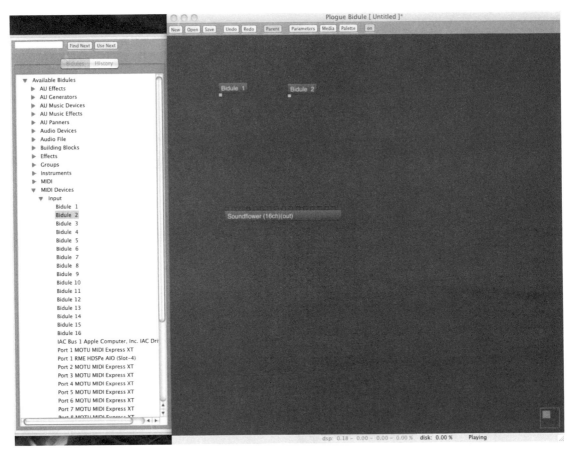

Figure 32.6   Plogue Bidule with the Soundflower audio device and two Bidule MIDI inputs.

5.   I click on the Instruments tab and drag the first three into the Kontakt 4 Multi and assign the outputs to st. 1–3. See Figure 32.9.

We could do more, but for now I am going to use this, so I close the palette and save the Bidule.

Setting Up Logic Pro 9 to Work with Plogue Bidule

This will be somewhat similar to setting up Logic Pro 9 properly to use with Kontakt 3.5 as a standalone. While ADAT Lightpipe routing with your audio device is my preferred method, for this tutorial we will use Soundflower as the audio device input and Built-In Audio as the output.

As I mentioned in the Kontakt tutorial, there are two good workflow approaches here. One method is to use the MIDI instruments to play in the parts and monitor the audio through audio tracks with the proper input assignments and input monitoring enabled or create input channel strips in the Environment, and the other is to utilize Logic Pro's external instrument. Since we did the latter in the Kontakt tutorial, I will do the former here.

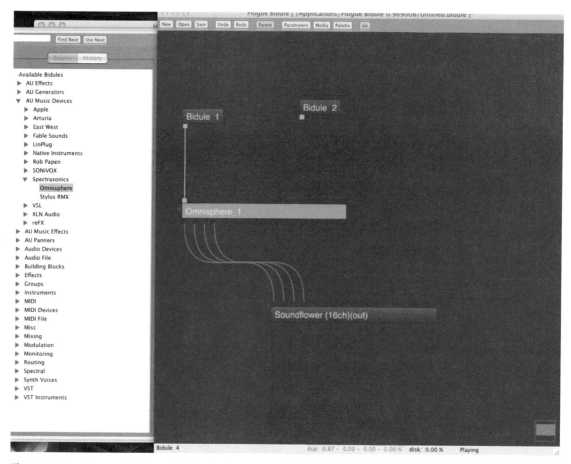

Figure 32.7 Plogue Bidule with Omnisphere properly cabled.

1.   Open a new project in Logic Pro from the Empty Project template and create two external MIDI instruments. (These are *not* the same thing as the software instrument named External that we used in the Kontakt tutorial.)

2.   In the Arrange window, there are now two tracks that actually belong to one multi instrument. To see what I am talking about, press Command+8 to open the Environment and navigate to the MIDI Instruments layer. Here you see a multi instrument named GM Device with all 16 MIDI channels enabled. Let's rename it Omnisphere using the Text tool. In the Inspector, change its MIDI port assignment from All to Bidule 1. See Figure 32.10.

3.   In the Devices tab, where you choose an audio interface, choose Built-In Output and Soundflower Input and click Apply Changes if you have not done so previously.

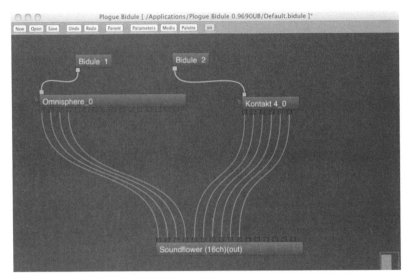

Figure 32.8   Plogue Bidule with Omnisphere and Kontakt 4 properly cabled.

Figure 32.9   Morphestra inside Kontakt 4 with three patches loaded and assigned to discrete outputs.

Figure 32.10   Assigning the Omnisphere multi instrument to Bidule 1.

4.   The next step is so *very important* that although I described this in the Kontakt 3.5 tutorial, I will describe it again here. Press Command+8 to open the Environment and navigate to the Clicks & Ports layer. Create an instrument (MIDI) and assign its port to Off. Name it Dead End or something similar. Draw a cable from the IAC Bus 1 on the Physical Output to the new instrument. This is to prevent the possibility of a MIDI feedback loop.

5.   Back in the Arrange window, simply click the + sign and create three more external MIDI instruments to address the three Silk patches in East West Play, right? Er…no. All that does is create tracks for the next subchannels of the Omnisphere multi instrument, which is frankly why I still prefer to manually create multi instruments in the Environment and only enable the subchannels I want to use. So in the MIDI instruments layer of the Environment, create a multi instrument, name it Morphestra, enable the first three subchannels, and reassign its MIDI port to Bidule 2. See Figure 32.11.

Now we need to get these tracks into the Arrange window's track list.

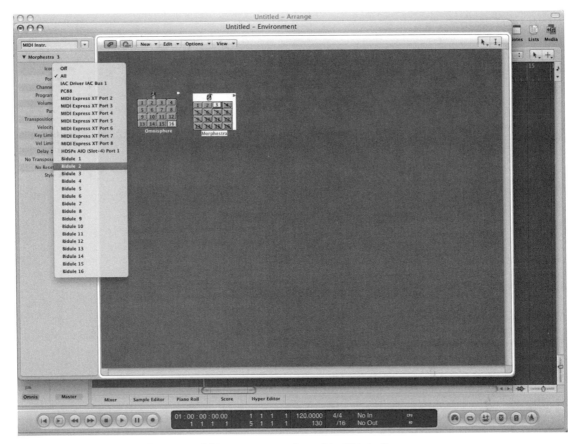

Figure 32.11 The Morphestra multi instrument assigned to Bidule 2.

6. Press X to open the Mixer, switch its view to All, and filter out everything except MIDI. On the right, you will see the three Morphestra multi instrument subchannels. Select them.

7. In the local Options menu, choose Create Arrange Tracks for Selected Channel Strips. See Figure 32.12.

    We now have created what we need to send MIDI to the software instruments in Plogue Bidule. Now we need to bring in the audio. Fortunately, in Logic Pro 9, it is easy.

8. Click the + sign and create five stereo audio tracks, each with input monitoring enabled, assigned to ascending inputs starting with Input 1-2.

Play the various MIDI instrument tracks, and you will hear the sounds and see the audio coming in on the audio tracks. The additional benefit of this methodology is that now if you want to record the MIDI as audio, you need only arm the audio tracks, hit Record, and away you go! See Figure 32.13.

Figure 32.12 Adding the Morphestra subchannels to the Arrange window.

Figure 32.13 The Mixer with the audio tracks armed and ready to record MIDI parts.

Index